Exploring Education Policy i World: Concepts, Contexts,

CW01083995

Series Editors

Eryong Xue, Faculty of Education, Beijing Normal University, Beijing, China

Simon Marginson, University of Oxford, Oxford, UK

Jian Li, Faculty of Education, Beijing Normal University, Beijing, China

This book series explores education policy on Pre-K, K-12, post-secondary education, and vocational education, informing multiple experts from academia to practitioner, and specifically pays focuses on new frontiers and cutting-edge knowledge that transforms future education policy development. It has been initiated by a global group of education policy research centers and institutions, whose faculty and staff includes internationally recognized researchers in comparative education policy studies. The series' mission is to advance the modernization of the education and social construction.

This series provides policymakers and researchers with an in-depth understanding of international education policy from diverse perspectives. Topics include cutting-edge and multidisciplinary studies on identifying, analyzing and uncovering education policy reform and practice among the fields in education policy and pedagogy. It addresses how education policy shapes the development of education systems in different regions and seeks to explain how specific education policies concentrate on accelerating the development of quality education and social progress. More importantly, this book series offers policymakers and educational stakeholders, government, and private sectors a comprehensive lens to investigate the trends, rationales of education policy development internationally.

More information about this series at http://www.springer.com/series/16621

Jian Li · Eryong Xue

"One Belt and One Road" and China's Education Development

A Policy Analysis Perspective

 Springer

Jian Li
Faculty of Education
Beijing Normal University
Beijing, China

Eryong Xue
Faculty of Education
Beijing Normal University
Beijing, China

Eryong Xue and Jian Li share the co-first authorship and contribute equally in this book.

The study received funding from Beijing Education Science Planning (Key project) Research on Internationalization Development Strategy and Evaluation Index System of Capital Universities under the Background of "Double First- Class" [No. AAAA19009].

ISSN 2730-6356   ISSN 2730-6364 (electronic)
Exploring Education Policy in a Globalized World: Concepts, Contexts, and Practices
ISBN 978-981-16-3270-9   ISBN 978-981-16-3268-6 (eBook)
https://doi.org/10.1007/978-981-16-3268-6

This Springer imprint is published by the registered company Springer Nature Singapore Pte Ltd.
The registered company address is: 152 Beach Road, #21-01/04 Gateway East, Singapore 189721, Singapore

Preface

In recent years, as China's "One Belt and One Road" initiative has become a broad international consensus and boosting international education has not only injected new momentum into international education aid, but also enriched the content of international education aid, expanded the new field of international education aid, and opened up a new model of international education aid. In his opening speech at the Roundtable of the First Belt and Road Forum for International Cooperation in May 2017, President Xi Jinping pointed out that "let the general public become the main force and beneficiaries of the development of the One Belt and One Road". Promoting the common prosperity of "One Belt and One Road" education to benefit the people is not only the need to strengthen mutually beneficial cooperation with other countries along the Belt and Road in education, but also the need to promote the reform and development of China's education. "One Belt and One Road" aims to promote the common development of countries along the routes, but also provides opportunities for regional education openness, exchange and integration.

Thus, this book aims to exploring how to promote "One Belt and One Road" Initiative for China's Education Development and what kinds of educational policy implementation in China's vocational education field, higher education system, and basic education system, locally and nationally. The policy analysis also is applied to uncover the overall landscape of promoting the construction of "One Belt and One Road" strategy in contemporary China. China is willing to work together to build a diversified and flexible educational cooperation mechanism through international education cooperation, taking connectivity as the basic requirement and the basic principle of wide consultation, joint contribution and sharing, so as to meet the mutually beneficial educational cooperation needs of all parties in "One Belt and One Road" countries and promote common educational development.

Chapter 1 concentrates on examining the macro-level education policy in "The Belt and Road" strategy. In particular, the policy text analysis of the macro-level education policy in "The Belt and Road" Strategy, the policy implementation analysis of the macro-level education policy in "The Belt and Road" Strategy, and the policy challenges analysis of the macro-level education policy in "The Belt and Road" Strategy have been offered in this chapter. In addition, the conclusion, suggestions and remarks have been provided in the last section.

Chapter 2 focuses on exploring promoting the implementation of "The belt and Road" strategy from a local practice policy analysis. The local provinces have issued to promote "area" initiative to implement the education policy. They take concrete actions to serve national initiative "area", and actively integrated into the "area" development, promote the development of high education quality, this article at the 18th party congress will comb, where the provinces of advancing along the "area" initiative to implement the education policy documents, summarizes the policy content characteristics, combined with the practice of education policy, summarizes the problems found, serve education better "area" initiative to provide policy recommendations.

Chapter 3 concentrates on examining the policy analysis of the implementation of "Belt and Road" imitative in China's vocational education. In recent years, China's higher vocational education has actively explored the path of overseas cooperation in running schools and served the construction of "One Belt and One Road". In practice, excellent cases such as Laban Workshop and Zhongshan Vocational and Technical College have been formed, and advanced experiences such as exerting industrial characteristics, participating in the construction in multiple ways and innovating the education mode have been accumulated. However, China's higher vocational colleges are still faced with various challenges from system mechanism to cooperation mode to enter the countries along the "Belt and Road", so it is still necessary to make joint efforts in various aspects to build the vocational education brand with Chinese characteristics.

Chapter 4 concentrates on exploring the policy analysis of higher education for "One Belt and One Road" imitative implementation. We provide intellectual support to the Belt and Road Initiative and establish an alliance of think tanks for research in countries along the Belt and Road. Build a "One Belt and One Road" resource and element sharing platform to promote multicultural communication. At the same time, the B&R countries are faced with the following challenges: diversified education systems, lack of experience in trans-regional cooperation in higher education, and insufficient supply of policy support; Cultural differences among countries along the Belt and Road are great, and there is an imbalance between the supply and demand of high-level personnel training. The promotion of bilateral and multilateral cooperation mechanisms of multi-parties needs to be strengthened. Different and diversified practice modes of higher education cooperation are insufficient, and the communication and cooperation ideas are limited. The level of higher education cooperation needs to be improved. The cross-border cooperation guarantee system for higher education is not sound, and the quality of cooperation needs to be improved. The implementation of higher education service "One Belt and One Road" initiative should improve the top-level design policy system, focus on the interaction and coordination mechanism of higher education, and improve the project certification standard system. Adhere to cultivate people by virtue, through the higher education service "One Belt and One Road" initiative major field action plan, the development of high-level international national talent training mode; For universities, it is necessary to strengthen the internal and external cooperation and improve the international cooperation system construction of the "Belt and Road" higher education.

Chapter 5 involves examining the policy analysis of "One Belt and One Road" initiatives in China's basic education system. The One Belt and One Road, as a new development background, is an important historical development opportunity for China. Since the One Belt and One Road was implemented, China and neighboring countries have achieved mutual benefits. The development of One Belt and One Road is inseparable from talents, and education is the main way to train people. Therefore, the One Belt and One Road cannot develop without education, and education also obtains a new chance under the One Belt and One Road development. On the one hand the number of students coming to China to continue to increase, on the other hand, China's education also gradually go abroad, basic education as the basis of the entire education work plays a foundation role, at present our country foundation education opening to the outside world expands unceasingly, there are some excellent primary and secondary schools abroad, overseas schools, spread the culture of education and educational experience, but at present the policy is not enough complete, will not be able to motivate some excellent schools abroad, so we need to complete the related policy, continue to push forward the process of basic education opening to the outside world.

Chapter 6 concentrates on exploring the policy analysis on the Belt and Road Initiative for students studying in China. Since China put forward the "One Belt and One Road" initiative in 2013, in addition to the cooperation in commercial trade, infrastructure construction and other aspects, the education cooperation with countries along the Belt and Road has also made great progress. This chapter takes 42 double first-class universities as the research objects, analyzes the policies of universities on studying in China, tries to find out the characteristics and experience patterns of universities' policies on studying in China from "One Belt and One Road" countries, and finally puts forward relevant suggestions.

Beijing, China

Jian Li
Eryong Xue

Acknowledgments Warmly thanks to the following contributors to collect data and materials: Tian Shixu, Shao Junjie, Qi Wenxin, Bo Yanling, Wang Xiao, and Lyu Ning.

Contents

About the Authors

Jian Li is the assistant professor in China Institute of Education Policy, Faculty of Education, Beijing Normal University. She received her Ph.D. degree in Educational Leadership and Policy Studies (ELPS), School of Education, Indiana University Bloomington. Her research interests focus on Education Policy Studies, Globalization and Internationalization of Higher Education. Dr. Li currently also serves as think tanker at China Institute of Education and Social Development, Beijing Normal University. In the past years, she has published more than 70 papers in *Chinese and English in Higher Education, International Journal of Education Research, Educational Philosophy and Theory, Educational Research, Comparative Education Research, China Education Journal and other SSCI and CSSCI indexed journals.* She has published 14 English monographs, participated in the editing of 2 English works, and published more than 20 articles in China Education Daily, People's Political Consultative Conference News and People's Daily Overseas Edition. More than 30 international academic conference papers, national, provincial and ministerial level decision-making departments adopted or participated in the writing of more than 20 proposals of the CPPCC National Committee. Presided over or participated in 6 national, provincial and ministerial projects and also serves as the editorial board member and reviewer of several international English journals.

Eryong Xue is the professor in China Institute of Education Policy, Faculty of Education, Beijing Normal University. Changjiang scholars (young scholars) awarded by the Ministry of Education in China. He is also a research fellow of the center for science and technology and education development strategy in Tsinghua university. He is also a postdoctoral fellow in the public administration of Tsinghua university. He has published more than 100 Chinese and English papers in the field of educational research. He has produced more than 100 CSSCI articles. He has won the seventh award for outstanding achievements in scientific research in institutions of higher learning, the fifth national award for outstanding achievements in educational scientific research, and the award for outstanding achievements in political participation and discussion by the central committee for the advancement of the people for more than 40 times. More than 40 independent or co-authored consulting reports were adopted by decision-making departments or approved by leaders. He has presided over more than 10 national or provincial projects such as national social science fund, natural science fund, ministry of education humanities and social science fund, Beijing philosophy and social science project, participated in 9 national or provincial key projects such as ministry of education philosophy and social science project, and 1 international cooperation project. The project of national natural science foundation of China was awarded excellent. He has been honored as the advanced worker of summer social practice for students at capital college and technical secondary school, the outstanding talent of Beijing division, the young talent of Beijing social science federation, the outstanding talent of Beijing universities and colleges, and the outstanding talent of Beijing. Main social part-time jobs: member of the 14th committee of the communist youth league of Beijing, deputy director of the working committee of college students and young teachers, special expert of China education association, China education development strategy society, national academic level office, director of Beijing postdoctoral fellowship (the 20th session).

Chapter 1
The Macro-Level Education Policy in "The Belt and Road" Strategy: A Policy Text Analysis

This chapter concentrates on examining the macro-level education policy in "The Belt and Road" strategy. In particular, the policy text analysis of the macro-level education policy in "The Belt and Road" Strategy, the policy implementation analysis of the macro-level education policy in "The Belt and Road" Strategy, and the policy challenges analysis of the macro-level education policy in "The Belt and Road" Strategy have been offered in this chapter. In addition, the conclusion, suggestions and remarks have been provided in the last section.

1.1 Introduction

In order to adapt to the world multiploidization and economic globalization, cultural diversity, the tide of social informatization, maintaining regional security and safety in China, realize the goal of the Chinese national rejuvenation, on September 7, 2013, Xi Jinping delivered an important speech, for the first time put forward strengthen policy communication, road, trade flow, currency, hearts are interlinked, work together for the silk road economic belt of the strategic initiatives. In his important speech to the Indonesian Parliament on October 3, 2013, President Xi Jinping stated clearly that China is committed to strengthening connectivity with various countries and is ready to develop sound maritime cooperative partnership with countries to jointly build the 21st Century Maritime Silk Road. Thus, the strategic conception of "One Belt and One Road" is presented in the world. At the Third Plenary Session of the 18th CPC Central Committee, the "One Belt and One Road" strategy was written into the *Decision of the CPC Central Committee on Several Major Issues of Comprehensively Deepening Reform*, which was officially elevated to the national strategy and became the strategic focus of China's new round of opening up and going global. In March 2014, Premier Li Keqiang pointed out in *the Government*

Work Report of the State Council that we need to speed up the planning and construction of the Silk Road Economic Belt and the 21st Century Maritime Silk Road. In 2015, *the State Council Government Work Report* also proposed to promote the construction of the Silk Road Economic Belt and the 21st Century Maritime Silk Road. "One Belt and One Road" construction has created a brand-new model for international cooperation in the twenty-first century and has become the "new business card" of China to show the atmosphere of great powers to the outside world, known as China's "second opening up". As General Secretary Xi Jinping pointed out, in promoting the "One Belt and One Road" construction, economic cooperation and cultural and people-to-people exchanges should be promoted together, and cultural and people-to-people exchanges in education, tourism, academia and art between China and B&R countries should be promoted to a new level. In this century's systematic project, education plays an important role and plays a basic and guiding role. Therefore, it is more important to shoulder the mission, promote educational exchanges and cooperation among countries along the Belt and Road, actively cultivate talents, adapt to and lead the construction of "One Belt and One Road" (Liu & Zhang, 2018; Teng et al., 2018; Zheng & Liu, 2016).

Along with above, this paper is divided into several parts to examine the macro-level education policy in "The Belt and Road" Strategy: the first part concentrates on the policy text analysis of the macro-level education policy in "The Belt and Road" Strategy; the second part focuses on the policy implementation analysis of the macro-level education policy in "The Belt and Road" Strategy, and the third part explores the policy challenges analysis of the macro-level education policy in "The Belt and Road" Strategy have been offered in this study. In addition, the conclusion, suggestions and remarks are offered in the last section.

1.2 The Policy Text Analysis of the Macro-Level Education Policy in "The Belt and Road" Strategy

1.2.1 Statistical Analysis of Policy Texts

In this study, the relevant macro-educational policy choices promulgated and implemented at the national level under the "One Belt and One Road" initiative were taken as the research objects, and data were obtained in two ways: First, the policy document database of the State Council was obtained. Based on the preliminary search results, the researchers screened the policy documents by manually searching and reviewing them one by one, combined with the established research objects in the earlier stage. In the public section of the home page of the Ministry of Education, the sub-column of important documents was locked, and relevant policy documents were screened out by searching the documents of the central government, the Ministry of Education and other departments one by one. Based on the above two data acquisition methods, 37 policy documents were finally selected as the analysis object (see the list of policy documents in the appendix at the end of the paper for details). First of all, from the perspective of time, the national macro education policies in the "One Belt and One Road" strategy mainly began to appear successively after 2013. In 2017 and 2018, the number of relevant policy documents was the highest, reaching 9 and 12 respectively. Secondly, from the perspective of institutional level, the Ministry of Education and other ministries and commissions account for the majority of policy documents, and the General Office of the CPC Central Committee and the General Office of the State Council jointly issued two policy documents.

1.2.2 Content Analysis of Policy Text

In terms of policy text content, mainly involving the exchange and cooperation in education, language education, language education, Chinese international education, etc., the internationalization of higher education/Chinese-foreign cooperation in running schools, vocational education internationalization, the student's education/student's education, education informatization, cross-border ethnic education, the content of patriotism education, personnel training, etc. In 2015, authorized by the State Council, the National Development and Reform Commission, the Ministry of Foreign Affairs, the Ministry of Commerce jointly issued to promote to build the silk road economic belt and the twenty-first century the vision and action of the Marine silk road (Ma, 2021; Song, 2021).

1.2.3 Policy Text Features

Focusing on opening up, inclusiveness and common development. In terms of the policy itself, opening up, peaceful development, joint contribution and shared benefits are the core concepts of the One Belt and One Road Initiative. Therefore, under the guidance of this concept, "openness", "development", "respect", "cooperation" and "win-win" have become the high-frequency words in relevant education policy texts of the "One Belt and One Road" strategy. China's foreign education cooperation under the "One Belt and One Road" initiative is an important way for countries along the Belt and Road to consolidate the foundation for development and deepen development. Most of the countries along the "One Belt and One Road" are developing countries and emerging economies, which have great needs in social infrastructure construction and talent training. In 2016, 41 countries along the Belt and Road were still on the list of recipients of Assistance from the Development Assistance Committee of the OECD, including eight least developed countries. Based on this, the "One Belt and One Road" initiative in the planning and practice reflects an obvious policy tilt to infrastructure construction. On the one hand, China's foreign education cooperation not only guarantees the development rights of the people of the countries along the Belt and Road by providing various forms of education assistance, but also opens special scholarship programs and cooperative education programs to broaden the development opportunities for the people of the countries along the Road. On the other hand, in serving countries, China has taken the initiative to meet the needs of countries along the Belt and Road and implemented educational cooperation in the consultation and construction of personnel training mechanism and people-to-people exchange mechanism urgently needed by countries along the Belt and Road.

Emphasizing the promotion of internationalization of education, especially higher education. The "One Belt and One Road" initiative crosses the Eurasian continent, covers Southeast Asia, Northeast Asia and finally leads to Europe through integration, forming the general trend of opening up and co-construction of the Eurasian continent. From the perspective of the policy text, China's foreign education cooperation under the "One Belt and One Road" initiative has communicated different practical levels of education internationalization, rather than being limited to the existing four levels. It has broken the boundary of time and space and formed a long-lasting educational cooperation pattern that connects land and sea geographically and has strong staying power in time. In addition, although the "area" under the initiative of China international education cooperation although involved from basic education to higher education cooperation and development of every stage of education, but objectively speaking, the higher education sector is still the present Chinese foreign education in key areas of cooperation, and that with the development of the internationalization tide of education center of gravity is also very consistent, "One Belt And One Road" initiative of foreign education cooperation in the field of higher education and higher education internationalization, that they are synthetic and two forces interact with each other. In addition, the internationalization of vocational education and the reform of personnel training in vocational education are also emphasized in the policy text (Liu & Zhang, 2018; Ma, 2021; Song, 2021; Teng et al., 2018; Zheng & Liu, 2016).

Emphasizing the promotion of cultural power. The One Belt and One Road initiative is facing serious challenges in both the cognitive and cultural fields of the international community. The complex cultural ecology of the countries along the Belt and Road, the concept of cultural centralism nourished by tradition and the nationalist trend caused by the rise of great powers all aggravate the cultural conflicts between China and other countries to different degrees. In addition, due to the lack of cross-cultural interpretation ability in China, western countries always adhere to a skeptical attitude based on the "Thucydides Trap" for China's development, deliberately misinterpret or even smear the real purpose of the "One Belt and One Road" initiative, comparing it to the "Chinese version of the Marshall Plan". How to properly deal with this series of thorny issues is not only the basic premise for the "One Belt and One Road" initiative to deepen development and the smooth development of education cooperation, but also the inevitable requirement for China to establish a good image in the international community. Therefore, based on the analysis of the policy text, it can be found that the education policy under the "One Belt and One Road" initiative actually reflects three orientations. First, it conveys the thinking spirit of "solidarity and mutual trust, equality and mutual benefit, inclusiveness and mutual learning, and win-win cooperation". Second, explain China's development philosophy of peaceful development and building a community with a shared future for mankind. Third, enhance the international competitiveness of domestic cultural products and open up the potential cultural market of countries along the "One Belt and One Road" (Ma, 2021; Song, 2021; Teng et al., 2018).

1.3   Policy Implementation Analysis of the Macro-Level Education Policy in "The Belt and Road" Strategy

Enriching the practice mode of educational cooperation and build multidimensional educational cooperation pattern. China's foreign education cooperation under the "One Belt and One Road" initiative is not only about study abroad plans or cooperation in running schools, but also multi-dimensional cooperation from policy to mechanism, from concept to practice. To be specific, it mainly includes the following four practical modes of foreign education cooperation: First, strategic education cooperation. Strategic education cooperation is an important link in the top-level design of China's foreign education cooperation, which is mainly driven by external factors such as international development trends and national development plans. In strategic education cooperation, the government is the most important participant, through the leading role of the government to promote education cooperation, to achieve the goal of enhancing the overall competitiveness of the country or region. As an important force leading the development trend of education cooperation under the "One Belt and One Road" initiative, strategic education cooperation not only needs to establish the direction in the overall development pattern, but also needs to gather strength in the implementation of the small pattern. The education cooperation under the "One Belt and One Road" initiative is an important strategic policy between governments at the macro level, but in practice, its strategic cooperation mode is mainly manifested in the policy communication construction and the public communication construction in education cooperation. Second, cooperation in service-oriented education. Service-oriented education cooperation is the foundation of the construction of "One Belt and One Road" initiative. Under the joint action of internal and external drivers, with the help of national policies, it accelerates the improvement of government service level and further enhances the accessibility of government services. With the purpose of serving the country, the people and the development, the service-oriented education cooperation aims to remove all kinds of obstacles in China's foreign education cooperation under the "One Belt and One Road" initiative and promote the far-reaching development of education cooperation. Compared with strategic educational cooperation, service-oriented educational cooperation pays more attention to solving specific difficulties in practice. Government, school and social forces are all important participants in this cooperation mode, but their roles and roles are different. In the interaction with the government, schools and social forces feedback the problems existing in educational cooperation, and with the help of policies and financial support provided by the government, schools play an active role as the executors of service-oriented education cooperation. Third, resource-based education cooperation. Resource-based education cooperation is mainly driven by internal motivation (Liu & Zhang, 2018; Ma, 2021; Song, 2021; Teng et al., 2018; Zheng & Liu, 2016).

Therefore, under the "Belt and Road" initiative, a series of key promotion plans for overseas study, cooperative school running, teacher training and joint training have been carried out in the field of education with talent cultivation as the main goal. Developmental educational cooperation is an important practice mode dominated by external motivation and acted on by internal and external motivation. Under the traction of external factors such as international development situation and national policy planning, combined with internal factors such as educational development needs, development-oriented education cooperation can realize the mutual benefit and win-win situation of national or regional development cooperation through the construction of cooperation mechanism among different cooperation subjects. In this mode, the government, schools and social forces form an important linkage mechanism among each other and promote the construction of many cooperative policy mechanisms and platforms through the interaction of different participants. One of the key points of education cooperation under the "One Belt and One Road" initiative is to build the Silk Road education cooperation mechanism, which is also the institutional guarantee to promote the cooperation and development of countries along the Silk Road.

Innovating the mechanism of educational exchange and work and build an effective carrier of key operations. Since the beginning of the new century, the educational exchanges between China and the countries along the Belt and Road have become increasingly frequent, and three sets of working mechanisms have been basically formed. The first is the decision-making mechanism, which has the functions of macro planning, coordination and consultation. With the mission of promoting the Chinese language and spreading Chinese culture, Confucius Institute has built a cultural bridge between China and the rest of the world. As of December 2015, a total of 500 Confucius Institutes and 1,000 Confucius Classrooms have been established around the world since the first Confucius Institute was established in South Korea in 2004. In South and Central Asian countries along the "One Belt and One Road" route, from 2005 to 2015, China set up 22 Confucius Institutes and 17 Confucius Classrooms with more than 10 other countries. The universities of the two countries have worked closely in teacher training, curriculum design, textbook compilation and student training, which has greatly promoted the countries along the Belt and Road to better understand and recognize Chinese culture. Among regional cooperation organizations, the SCO University, which was established in August 2007, provides a new platform for exchanges and cooperation. Thanks to the joint efforts of the member states, steady progress has been made in various aspects of the SCO University, including its organizational principles, coordination mechanisms, project institutions, administrative bodies, enrollment procedures and training programs. At present, the number of project institutions has increased to 76, including 20 Chinese schools and 56 foreign schools. The priority is to train talents in regional science, ecology, energy science, IT, nanotechnology, economics, education and other disciplines.

Building a platform for educational exchanges and dialogue to expand the space for foreign cooperation. China has set up 123 Confucius Institutes and 50 Confucius Classrooms in One Belt and One Road countries, accounting for 24.6% and 0.05% of the total number of Confucius Institutes and Classrooms in the world, respectively, in 47 countries. There are 200 cooperation programs and institutions in China from countries along the Belt and Road, accounting for nearly 1/10 of the total projects in China, and 8 countries involved, accounting for 12% of the total number of "One Belt and One Road" countries. China's cooperation in running schools in Belt and Road countries includes Xiamen University in Malaysia, Soochow University in Laos, and Yunnan University of Finance and Economics Bangkok Business School. There are more than 90 cooperation programs in 14 countries and regions. At the same time, since the "One Belt and One Road" initiative was put forward, more than 10 countries, including Pakistan, Kazakhstan, Jordan and Egypt, have submitted applications for overseas education to China. At the beginning of 2015, Jordanian Prime Minister Mashir invited Chinese colleges and universities to carry out vocational education in Jordan and train applied talents for Jordan. China's education is opening its mind to the world as never before, making a unique contribution to building a community with a shared future for mankind and creating a better future for the world (Liu & Zhang, 2018; Ma, 2021; Song, 2021; Teng et al., 2018; Zheng & Liu, 2016).

1.4 Policy Challenges Analysis of the Macro-Level Education Policy in "The Belt and Road" Strategy

Challenges posed by the complex international political and economic environment. The political and economic landscape of the world today is complex and volatile. The trend toward a multi-polar world, economic globalization and regional economic integration is gaining momentum. All kinds of global problems are becoming more prominent. In the field of international politics, the situation of "one super and many powers" continues to exist. With the strong rise of emerging powers such as China and India, the balance of power among countries is further developing in the direction of equalization, and the trend of world multi-polarization is becoming more obvious. In addition, the international influence of developing countries in Asia, Africa and Latin America is constantly rising. Major powers and emerging powers have adjusted their domestic and foreign policies in response to new changes in the international situation. Their interactions have become more active and competition in overall national strength has intensified. In the field of international economy: Since the beginning of the new century, the world economic landscape has stepped into a new stage of major turbulence, major adjustment and major transformation. "Uncertainties and destabilizing factors are on the rise in world economic growth, profound changes are under way in global trade and investment patterns and capital flows, and countries in Asia and Europe are at a critical stage of economic transformation and upgrading, with their economic development facing varying degrees of difficulties and challenges." In the field of international security: Traditional and non-traditional security threats have long coexisted, and the social security situation has shown a new trend of development. The "three forces" of terrorism, separatism and extremism are active in Eurasia. Border and territorial disputes have led to local conflicts from time to time, and the involvement of major countries has made regional hotspot issues more complicated. Maritime disputes between countries along the "Maritime Silk Road" have also been unresolved for a long time. Non-traditional security threats, such as energy and resource shortages, natural disasters, infectious diseases, information networks, arms proliferation, environmental degradation, drug trafficking, illegal migration and transnational crimes, are on the rise. The above factors are often intertwined, seriously affecting the peace and stability of the countries and regions along the Belt and Road, causing unnecessary estrangement and friction, and posing severe challenges to the implementation of the "One Belt and One Road" strategy.

The cultural differences among different nationalities and the challenge of religious infiltration. The diversity of ethnic groups, the complexity of religions and the concomitant cultural differences all pose challenges to educational exchanges and cooperation among countries along the Belt and Road. However, the religious beliefs of Central Asia, South Asia and other countries adjacent to China's border are relatively complex, which makes the western region the front line of foreign religious infiltration, thus increasing the instability and uncertainty factors in China's border areas. In short, with the advancement of the "One Belt and One Road" strategy, the cultural and educational exchanges between China and countries along the Belt and Road are becoming increasingly frequent. How to prevent the infiltration and destruction of ethnic separatist forces, properly handle religious issues and safeguard national sovereignty is a major challenge that cannot be ignored (Ma, 2021; Song, 2021; Zheng & Liu, 2016).

Challenges arising from differences in educational systems between different countries and regions. There are differences between capitalist countries and socialist countries, developed countries and developing countries, big countries and small countries along the "One Belt and One Road". Therefore, based on different national conditions, their education systems are also quite different. Take the five Central Asian countries as an example. As the republics of the former Soviet Union, the education of the five Central Asian countries was deeply influenced by the Soviet education model. With the political transformation and economic transformation, the education system of these five countries has undergone new changes. The state actively encourages private education to change the situation that public education dominates the world. Kazakhstan, for example, had 112 private schools out of 170 higher education institutions as early as 2001. In 2013, Kazakhstan's minister of education, science and technology announced: "Most regions will have one state university and one private university." The proportion of private schools in secondary vocational education has also remained above 55%. The transformation and transformation of the educational system, to a great extent, affects the development of educational exchanges and cooperation. In addition, because education in different countries is at different stages of development, and each country has different teaching levels, faculty, superior disciplines and key research areas, a lot of preparatory work needs to be done when carrying out educational exchanges and cooperation. Due to the differences in education systems, there are many obstacles in the mutual recognition of courses, credits, academic qualifications and other aspects.

Challenges arising from insufficient awareness of the importance of educational exchange and cooperation. The importance of educational exchange and cooperation is not well understood. Since the introduction of the "One Belt and One Road" strategic conception, the domestic provinces and cities have shown great enthusiasm. The concepts of "starting point", "bridgehead", "core area", "free trade zone" and "hub" have been put forward one after another. Relevant provinces and cities all hope to seize the policy opportunities and seize the development opportunities, but this enthusiasm is mostly focused on the economic field, and there is an obvious lack of awareness of the importance of cultural and educational exchanges with countries along the Belt and Road. Internationally, there are still doubts about the promotion of educational exchanges and cooperation. Due to the political, legal and cultural differences among countries along the "One Belt and One Road", countries have different expectations for promoting educational exchanges and cooperation. Since the "One Belt and One Road" strategy was put forward, more than 30 countries, including Russia, Italy, South Korea and other countries have made clear statements. They may give "positive evaluation", "high praise", or "willing to actively participate", or "are considering and intend to cooperate". But India, a key player in the "Maritime Silk Road", has been lukewarm. This shows that some countries are wary of carrying out cultural and educational exchanges. On the one hand, they hope to develop their own education and cultivate much-needed talents with the help of Chinese funds, but on the other hand, they are afraid of becoming more dependent on China (Liu & Zhang, 2018; Ma, 2021; Song, 2021; Teng et al., 2018; Zheng & Liu, 2016).

1.5 Suggestions and Remarks

Strengthen top-level design and enhance high-level communication. First, we need to strengthen top-level design and strategic deployment. In combination with the formulation of the education plan of the 14th Five-Year Plan, we should make a good education policy planning that is compatible with the One Belt and One Road strategy. The strategic planning of education development corresponding to the "One Belt and One Road" strategy is regarded as a relatively independent field of strategic planning of education development. Combined with the formulation of national and regional "14th Five-Year" education plans, comprehensive and targeted planning and top-level design are carried out. To focus on the "One Belt and One Road" oriented talent training plan; We will focus on the planning of educational and scientific research for the Belt and Road Initiative. Focus on social service planning oriented to "One Belt and One Road"; We will focus on the cultural and educational communication planning for the Belt and Road Initiative. It is necessary to deal with the local and overall relationship between the "One Belt and One Road" education policy planning and the national and regional "14th Five-Year" education planning. In addition, the central government has a clear plan for the development of the "Silk Road Economic Belt", but there is still a lack of macro and systematic consideration in the aspects of cultural exchanges and educational cooperation. In the period to come, we need to vigorously promote people-to-people and cultural exchanges and educational cooperation. To promote the "One Belt and One Road" construction, we need to realize the "five links", among which the "people-to-people connectivity" mainly depends on people-to-people exchanges and educational cooperation.

Enrich cultural and people-to-people exchanges to enhance mutual understanding and trust. We need to focus on promoting the "Silk Road" overseas study, cooperation in running schools, teacher training, talent joint training and education assistance programs, promote the communication and mutual recognition of policies, channels, languages, people's hearts and academic credentials, and earnestly give play to the basic and leading role of education in the joint construction of "One Belt and One Road". At the same time, we should further strengthen the mechanism of cultural exchanges between China and other countries along the Belt and Road. By carrying out activities such as "demonstration teaching" and "mathematics textbooks" to go global, we should give full play to the advantages of China's basic education and show the characteristics and connotations of China's basic education to the outside world. In addition, the series of "Study Tour in China", "Study in China" and "Experience in China" can be launched in combination with various forms of cultural exchange, so as to form a stable international cognition among target countries and target groups, thus improving the efficiency of resource utilization and enhancing international reputation.

We also should enhance international understanding. It is important to further realize that how to dispel the doubts of other countries, create an environment conducive to the leading role of One Belt and One Road, and get the understanding and support of all parties is the key. Under the framework of international cooperation, education should attach importance to the development of international understanding education. International understanding education is to face up to the differences between different countries and nations, respect diverse values and cultures, and promote mutual understanding among different cultures. Therefore, international understanding education should be reflected in domestic and foreign school running and educational exchange programs, so that students can have a deep understanding of the society and culture of other countries and foreign students can have a more vivid understanding of China. In the future, China should learn from the international experience, strengthen the initiative in public opinion, deeply explore and strengthen the expression of public opinion value in education, and guide the world to know the real China. A rising China needs to tell the "China story" to the world, and the "China story" needs to be a strong theory of convincing, in addition to our own profound cultural heritage and confidence, the "China story" should be told by foreign people who understand Chinese culture and identify with Chinese values. Whether the Chinese nation can continuously cultivate foreign intellectual elites and people from all walks of life who know, are friendly to and friendly to China is crucial to whether the Chinese nation can continue to tell the "China story" to the world.

Deepen cross-border inter-university cooperation and explore new models of cooperation. "One Belt and One Road" strategy is a strategic conception with the main purpose of promoting economic prosperity and regional economic cooperation along the routes.

Extensive research on education, culture, history and policies of the countries along the Belt and Road and relevant countries should be carried out as well as related educational and cultural exchanges and cooperation. On the one hand, we have a comprehensive understanding of the basic situation of countries along the Belt and Road, and on the other hand, we have actively introduced China's achievements and experience in education, culture and historical development to those countries along the Road. Compared with economic exchanges, educational and cultural exchanges have a "soft" aspect. We can give priority to educational exchanges and cooperation to provide public support for the implementation of the "One Belt and One Road" strategy and open up a broader space for cooperation. At the same time, we should draw lessons from previous educational and cultural exchanges and cooperation between countries, constantly improve the ways of educational and cultural exchanges and cooperation and form new thinking and new ways of educational and cultural exchanges that match the "One Belt and One Road" strategy. We should encourage local governments to actively strengthen exchanges with countries along the Belt and Road and promote educational exchanges and cooperation at various levels, in various fields and in various forms. Promoting educational and cultural exchanges through governmental cooperation; Promote economic cooperation and trade through educational exchanges (Liu & Zhang, 2018; Ma, 2021; Song, 2021; Teng et al., 2018; Zheng & Liu, 2016).

References

Liu, B., & Zhang, W. (2018). Cultural conflicts and idea bridges—On the new world citizenship education under the background of "One Belt and One Road". *Education Research of Tsinghua University, 3* 9(4), 56–63.

Ma, W. (2021). "One Belt and One Road" initiative and internationalization transformation of higher education in China. *Journal of Beijing University of Aeronautics and Astronautics (Social Science Edition), 34*(1), 134–142.

Song, J. (2021). Exploration on the international cooperation and exchange of higher vocational colleges under the new situation. *Chinese Journal of Multimedia and Network Instruction (Medium Issue), 20*(1), 176–178.

Teng, J., Ding, R., Chen, L., & Wang, Y. (2018). Research on the education assistance pattern of countries along the "One Belt and One Road"—Based on the analysis of the official data of the development assistance committee in recent ten years. *Comparative Education Research, 40*(4), 10–19.

Zheng, G., & Liu, J. (2016). Dilemma and countermeasures of educational exchange and cooperation in "One Belt and One Road". *Strategy Comparative Education Research, 38*(2), 20–26.

Chapter 2
Promoting the Implementation of "The Belt and Road" Strategy: A Local Practice Policy Analysis

This chapter focuses on exploring promoting the implementation of "The belt and Road" strategy from a local practice policy analysis. The local provinces have issued to promote "area" initiative to implement the education policy. They take concrete actions to serve national initiative "area", and actively integrated into the "area" development, promote the development of high education quality, this article at the 18th party congress will comb, where the provinces of advancing along the "area" initiative to implement the education policy documents, summarizes the policy content characteristics, combined with the practice of education policy, summarizes the problems found, serve education better "area" initiative to provide policy recommendations.

2.1 Introduction

In March 2015, the Chinese government promulgated the drive and the silk road economic belt and the maritime silk road in the twenty-first century vision and action, defines "neighborhood" all the way along the route of the 18 provinces (autonomous regions), including Xinjian, Shaanxi, Gansu, Mingxia, Qinghai, Inner Mongolia and northwest of the six provinces of Heilongjiang, Jilin, Liaoning, northeast three provinces, and other three provinces of southwest guanxi, Yunnan, Tibet, Shanghai, Fujian, Guangdong, Zhejiang, Hainan province, are Chongqing inland areas. According to the special location advantage, Xinjian, Fujian as the core "area", taking "neighborhood" all the way the important role of transshipment hub, July 13, 2016, issued by the Ministry of Education about the push to build "area" education action (teach [2016] no. 46), for the new era of education service "area" pointed out the direction of the initiative, in November 2016, the Ministry of Education and Fujian, guanxi, Hainan, Guizhou, Yunnan, Xinjian six provinces (area) signed in Beijing the "area" education action international cooperation memorandum, in April 2017, The Ministry of Education, Inner Mongolia, Jilin, Heilongjiang, Shaanxi,

J. Li and E. Xue, *"One Belt and One Road" and China's Education Development*, Exploring Education Policy in a Globalized World: Concepts, Contexts, and Practices, https://doi.org/10.1007/978-981-16-3268-6_2

Qinghai, Qingdao and other six provinces (autonomous regions), signed in Beijing to carry out the "One Belt And One Road" education action international cooperation memorandum. For the implementation of the Ministry of Education, promote to build "area" education campaign, according to the general office of the central committee of the communist party of China and the State Council general office on the do a good job of education in the new period open several opinions, about to strengthen and improve the work of the Chinese and foreign cultural exchanges several opinions of the relevant documents spirit, the provinces (autonomous regions) in combination with the practical situation of the local education, have issued the policy document, for the new era of education service area initiative put forward concrete measures to step on the level of practice, a solid and effective to promote the healthy development of area initiative (Cao, 2020; Chen & Xu, 2020; Dong & Wu, 2018; Pan, 2019).

2.1.1   Policy Content

Of in-depth understanding of China's 31 provinces, municipalities, autonomous regions) levels of government to carry out the Ministry of Education "promote to build" area "education campaign", for China's 31 provinces, municipalities, autonomous regions) levels of government to establish the education service "area" initiative policy document to comb, policy documents from provinces (autonomous regions) of the people's government and education department website, in order to ensure the "area" typicality and the accuracy of policy document selection, screening policy strictly follow the following two principles:

First, the papers issued by units below the provincial and municipal levels are not counted. Second, the key words in the title and body of the policy document focus on the "One Belt, One Road", education, the New Silk Road Economic Belt and the (Maritime) Silk Road, etc., requiring the text to explicitly mention the content of the education services "One Belt and One Road" initiative. In addition to Tibet and Sichuan, the other 29 provinces and municipalities (autonomous regions) have all issued policy documents on education service "One Belt and One Road" initiative, with a total of 72 education policy documents.

2.1.2   The Characteristics of the Policy Text

Through sorting out the key contents of education policies in the implementation of the "One Belt And One Road" initiative in 31 provinces, municipalities (autonomous regions) in China, the following characteristics are found: Is a provincial, city, municipality) can actively will "area" initiative education service content into the relevant policy documents, some provinces and cities (autonomous regions) establish a participate in the plan of the construction of the "region", education services within the file "area" initiative measures to carry on the deployment schedule, some provinces and cities (autonomous regions) in the new education career development planning, can actively seize the great opportunities, "area" initiative to education career development and advancing the "area" initiative, on the one hand, raising the level of education internationalization development in the region, On the other hand, cultivate professional talents to serve the "One Belt And One Road" initiative, and actively participate in the deveined Belt and One Road of the "BBB1" initiative. All 31 provinces and municipalities (autonomous regions) (except Tibet and Sichuan) have issued policy documents related to the "One Belt and One Road" initiative of education services. Shaanxi Province has issued 7 relevant documents since 2015, and hone Belt and One Reemployed the "BBB2" initiative of education services in the annual One Belt And One Radon plan of "BBB1" construction every year. Second is worked out to promote "neighborhoods" initiative to implement the education policy of file balanced education practice, this area focused policies of text, the 72 documents issued by the 31 provinces, involved the content of the education service "area" initiative focuses on: education exchanges and cooperation, Chinese-foreign cooperation in running schools, vocational education cooperation, not general language teaching, the Confucius institute (class) construction, grant aid, two-way study of this a few aspects, and each province, city (autonomous regions) in combination with the practical situation of the local education, to promote the practice of "area" initiative focused policy file, such as: Guizhou province pays attention to strengthening the teaching development of non-common languages, Qinghai province pays attention to two-way study abroad in education, Yunnan province pays attention to international exchange and cooperation in vocational education, and all provinces, municipalities (autonomous regions) have made all-round arrangements for the education service "One Belt And One Road" initiative. Three is 31 provinces (autonomous regions) propulsion system introduced by the implementation of the "area" initiative education policy document number difference is big, main performance in Shaanxi province and Chongqing city establish the advance of "area" initiative to implement the policy document number is more, in Shaanxi province issued seven files, Chongqing introduced 6 files, and most of the other provinces and cities (autonomous regions) to establish the number of documents issued for about 1–4, Tibet and Sichuan have no corresponding policy documents. The policy content of Chongqing Municipality puts forward for the first time the implementation of the promotion of high-quality intelligent education results in colleges and universities and the promotion of intelligent education "going out", while the policy content of other provinces (autonomous regions) does not have this content (Cao, 2020; Chen & Xu, 2020; Ding, 2017; Dong & Wu, 2018; Feng, 2018; Lan, 2017; Pan, 2019; Ye, 2020; Yen, 2020; Zhang, 2017).

2.1.3 Policy Implementation

Since the national Ministry of Education issued "promote to build" area "education campaign", since the national provinces, municipalities, autonomous regions) actively establish advance "area" initiative to implement education policy documents, and actively into the action of the "area" initiative, profound grasp the "area" initiative will bring great opportunities, in combination with the practical situation of education in our region, targeted to develop the education development planning, Put forward to strengthen the exchanges and cooperation education, Chinese-foreign cooperation in running schools, the Confucius institute (class) construction, the internationalization of vocational education development, the general language teaching development, and support two-way study abroad, to strengthen the construction of think tank and a series of education development, has made remarkable achievements, to promote the "area" initiative injected with strong driving force, as well as "area" all the way along the country's education development to provide strong support.

Educational cooperation in running schools has achieved remarkable results. Through the collation of the relevant information of Chinese-foreign cooperatively-run schools and projects with undergraduate degrees and above updated by the Information Platform for the Supervision of Chinese-foreign Cooperation in Running Schools of the Ministry of Education of the People's Republic of China on December 1, 2020, it is found that there are a total of 1246 Chinese-foreign cooperatively-run schools and projects with undergraduate degrees and above, including 134 institutions and 1112 projects. According to the updated information of Chinese-foreign cooperative-running institutions and projects at undergraduate and above level updated on December 1, 2020 by the Supervision Information Platform of the Ministry of Education of the People's Republic of China on Chinese-foreign cooperative-running institutions and projects, it is found that there are 1,000 institutions and projects at undergraduate level and 306 institutions and projects at master level in terms of education level. According to the information platform of supervision of Chinese-foreign cooperation in running schools of the Ministry of Education, the number of Chinese-foreign cooperation in running schools and projects between China and countries along the "Belt and Road" takes up more than 10% of the total number of Chinese-foreign cooperation in running schools and projects and shows an increasing trend year by year. This shows that Chinese universities are actively responding to the national "One Belt and One Road" initiative and constantly strengthening the higher education cooperation with the count One Belt and One Road along the "BBB1". Among the countries along the "One Belt and One Road" that have cooperated with China in running schools, Russia has the largest number of institutions and projects with China, while Poland and Ukraine rank second and third. From the regional distribution, China and southeast Asia, Singapore, Thailand, Malaysia, India in South Asia, west Asia and north Africa the United Arab Emirates, Israel, Greece, in central and eastern Poland, Bulgaria, Hungary, Ukraine and Belarus and other countries have carried out cooperation in running schools, and the five central Asian countries not to carry out the cooperation in running schools.

The construction of Confucius Institutes (Classrooms) has made steady progress. Confucius institute is a non-profit established Sino-foreign cooperative education institutions, to adapt to the world countries (regions) of the people's need for Chinese learning, promote the countries all over the world (region) of the people's understanding of Chinese language and culture, strengthen the education and cultural exchanges and cooperation with the countries all over the world, the development of friendly relations between China and foreign, promote the development of the world cultural diversity, the construction of a harmonious world. Confucius Institutes carry out exchanges and cooperation in Chinese language teaching, education and culture between China and foreign countries. The services provided include Chinese language teaching; Train Chinese teachers and provide Chinese teaching resources; Carrying out Chinese language tests and Chinese teacher certification; Provide information consultation on Chinese education and culture; Carrying out language and cultural exchanges between China and foreign countries. Confucius Institutes in various regions have made full use of their advantages to carry out colorful teaching and cultural activities, and gradually formed a school-running model with their own characteristics. They have become an important place for countries to learn the Chinese language and culture and learn about contemporary China and are warmly welcomed by all sectors of the local society (Ding, 2017; Feng, 2018; Lan, 2017; Pan, 2019; Ye, 2020; Yen, 2020; Zhang, 2017).

According to the Hanban website (www.hanban.org), Confucius Institute is a non-profit educational institution jointly founded by China and foreign countries. Its purpose is to provide the world with a platform for learning Chinese language and culture, build a bridge for international communication and communication, and promote friendly exchanges and diversified development of cultures around the world. Since its establishment, Confucius Institutes have cultivated a large number of foreign friends who love Chinese language and culture, and attracted a number of outstanding scholars, becoming the most representative institutions for the international dissemination of Chinese language with their unique operation mechanism and educational mode. Up to now, 541 Confucius Institutes and 1,170 Confucius Classrooms have been set up in 162 countries and regions. Among them, 39 Asian countries (regions) have 135 Confucius Institutes and 115 Confucius Classrooms. There are 61 Confucius Institutes and 48 Confucius Classrooms in 46 African countries. There are 187 Confucius Institutes and 346 Confucius Classrooms in 43 countries (regions) in Europe. There are 138 Confucius Institutes and 560 Confucius Classrooms in 27 countries in the Americas. There are 20 Confucius Institutes and 101 Confucius Classrooms in seven countries of Oceania. In terms of total volume, Europe and America have the most Confucius Institutes and Classrooms, indicating the significant improvement of China's economic strength and cultural strength.

In terms of the number of Confucius Institutes established in different countries, combined with relevant data from the Xinhua Silk Road Network (www.imsilkroad. com), the situation of Confucius Institutes set up in 65 countries along the "One Belt and One Road" route is sorted out, as shown in the following table. It can be seen that 53 of the 65 B&R countries have set up 155 Confucius Institutes, accounting for 81% of the total. Russia has the largest number of Confucius Institutes (19), followed by Thailand (16). In the past two years, Russia, Slovakia, Bosnia and Herzegovina, Laos, Hungary, Malaysia, Cambodia, India, Belarus and other countries added more. On October 25, 2019, at the China-Pakistan Business Forum, the Confucius Institute

Headquarters and the Federal University of Goyas signed the Agreement on the Cooperative Establishment of the Confucius Institute of Traditional Chinese Medicine at the Federal University of Goyas in Brazil, marking the establishment of the 155th Confucius Institute along the One Belt and One Road (Cao, 2020; Ding, 2017; Dong & Wu, 2018; Yen, 2020).

As of October 2018, Xinjian university with Russia, Kyrgyzstan, Tajikistan, Kazakhstan, Pakistan, Mongolia and other colleges and universities cooperation of countries along the silk road economic belt built 10 Confucius institutes, there are 21 Confucius classrooms and nearly "in" the journal of Karamay a school in 2020, the cumulative registered students 133000 people, the cumulative Chinese culture dissemination activities of more than 3300 times. In order to support the work of the Confucius Institute, the autonomous region has trained more than 2,000 international Chinese language teachers and volunteers in recent years and sent 1,000 Chinese language teachers and 400 volunteers to teach abroad through different channels. Gansu universities have set up five Confucius Institutes and one Confucius Classroom abroad to actively promote Chinese language abroad, providing a good language communication environment for the "One Belt and One Road" construction. According to statistics, by 2017, not only 12 universities in Liaoning had set up nearly 24 Confucius Institutes in 20 countries around the world. On the basis of the Confucius Institutes all over the world today, we devote ourselves to inheriting and carrying forward the excellent culture of the Chinese nation, and actively promote the convergence and integration of Chinese and foreign cultures.

The scale of international students in China keeps expanding. Since the "One Belt And One Road" initiative was put forward, the overall scale of the education development of international students in B&R countries has been expanding, the source of students is concentrated, the source distribution of students of different learning categories, the distribution of learning levels and the distribution of professional needs are unbalanced, and the source of students' funding is mainly self-funded. First, the overall scale of international students in China is constantly expanding. In terms of absolute size, from 2013 to 2018, the number of international students from countries along the Belt and Road continued to rise, from 140,000 in 2013, 170,000 in 2014, 180,000 in 2015 and 210,000 in 2016 to 260,000 in 2018, with an average annual growth rate of 12.8%. During the same period, the global average annual growth rate of international students was 6.7%, a difference of 6 percentage points, and the growth momentum of international students from countries along the Belt and Road was obvious. In terms of relative size, the number of international students from B&R countries has been increasing in proportion to the total number of international students in the world, and they have become the main source of international students in the world. In 2013, there were 140,000 international students from countries along the Belt and Road and 360,000 from all over the world, accounting for 40% of the total. In 2018, 260,000 international students from countries along the Belt and Road and 490,000 from all over the world came to China, accounting for 53% of international students from countries along the Belt and Road, up 13% from 2013. In 2018, the number of foreign students in the top ten countries are South Korea,

Thailand, Pakistan, India, the United States, Russia, Indonesia, Laos, Japan, Kazakhstan, along the country accounted for 70%, students in China's top ten provinces and cities are Beijing, Shanghai, Jiangsu, Zhejiang, Liaoning, Tianjin, Guangdong, Hubei, Yunnan, Shandong province, more than 10000 provinces (area) and guanxi, Sichuan, Heilongjiang, Shaanxi, Fujian; Second, the distribution of students is more concentrated. The sources of international students in B&R countries are mainly in Southeast Asia, South Asia, Central Asia and Northeast Asia. From 2013 to 2018, the average proportion of international students in these regions in the total number of international students in B&R countries is 40.5, 21.86, 12.4, and 4.4%, respectively. Among them, students from Southeast Asia occupy the main position, but the growth rate is not large in recent years, with an average annual growth rate of 7.7%. South Asia saw the largest increase in international students, with an average annual growth rate of 44.4%. West Asia, North Africa, Central and Eastern Europe and other regions have great potential for growth in the number of international students. The concentration of the origin places of international students in the countries along the Belt and Road is also reflected in the concentration of the countries of origin. From 2013 to 2018, Thailand, Pakistan, India, Russia, Indonesia, Laos, Kazakhstan, Malaysia, Mongolia and Bangladesh are the top 10 countries in terms of the number of international students coming to China from B&R countries. In 2018, the number of foreign students from these 10 countries accounted for 66% of all foreign students from B&R countries. Third, the distribution of overseas students' learning categories, learning levels and professional needs is not balanced. From the perspective of learning types, the source places of overseas students in B&R countries are unbalanced for academic education (junior college, undergraduate, master/doctoral) and non-academic education (ordinary advanced students, advanced students, short-term overseas students). From 2013 to 2018, the majority of foreign students from Mongolia and 8 South Asian countries received academic education. The average number of Mongolian students with degrees accounted for about 70% of the total number of foreign students in Mongolia, and the average number of students with degrees from 8 South Asian countries accounted for about 87% of the total number of foreign students in China. In Southeast Asia, five countries in Central Asia and 19 countries in West Asia and North Africa, the number of foreign students receiving academic and non-academic education is relatively balanced, accounting for about 50% of the total number of foreign students in each country. In the 22 Central and Eastern European countries, the majority of international students receive non-degree education, with the number of non-degree students accounting for more than 60% of the total number of international students in the region. From the perspective of learning level, undergraduate students from countries along the Belt and Road are the majority. The proportion of undergraduate students from Mongolia, 10 countries in Southeast Asia, 8 countries in South Asia, 5 countries in Central Asia, 19 countries in West Asia and North Africa, and 22 countries in Central and Eastern Europe is between 40 and 85%. Followed by graduate students, accounting for between 17 and 56%; Junior college students are the least, the highest proportion of less than 10%. The number of non-degree students in China is mainly for general study, accounting for between 40 and 80% of the total number of non-degree students in

China. It is followed by short-term study and advanced study. The number of short-term study students accounts for 19–50% of the total number of non-degree students in China, and the proportion of advanced study students is less than 5%. This shows that the proportion of postgraduate and advanced students in international students from B&R countries needs to be increased, and the education of high-level students' needs to be strengthened. From the perspective of professional demand, international students from countries along the Belt and Road mainly study Chinese. Some majors related to the "One Belt and One Road" initiative, such as information and communication, engineering technology, computer science, electronic information engineering, etc., have not received wide attention and the number of students is not large. The construction of "One Belt and One Road" is still in its initial development stage. The education of international students in B&R countries mostly starts from Chinese teaching. With the continuous advancement of the construction process and the increasing demand for professional talents, the number of international students studying technical majors will also increase accordingly. Fourth, the main source of funds for international students is self-funded. In terms of the number of students, the number of students with scholarships in countries along the Belt and Road is significantly lower than the number of students with self-financing, and the number of students with self-financing is more than 5 times that of students with scholarships in years past. The proportion of self-funded students in the total number of international students from B&R countries has been around 85%, and in 2014 it was as high as 88%. However, the proportion of self-funded students decreased year by year, while the proportion of scholarship students increased year by year. In terms of growth rate, the number of students studying on scholarships and self-funded projects in B&R countries increased from 17,965 and 124,496 in 2013 to 40,635 and 219,989 in 2018, with an average annual growth rate of 17.7 and 12.1%, respectively. The growth rate of students studying on scholarships is significantly higher than that of self-funded students (Cao, 2020; Chen & Xu, 2020; Ding, 2017; Dong & Wu, 2018; Feng, 2018; Lan, 2017; Pan, 2019; Ye, 2020; Yen, 2020; Zhang, 2017).

In recent years, relying on the Ministry of Education of Fujian agriculture and forestry university Chinese government scholarship students in China accept this platform, positively facing southeast Asia and Africa and other countries along the sea silk to recruit foreign students, from 2013 to 2017 students in school has been increased by a factor of two, students from countries increased from 15 countries to 49 countries, including master accounts for more than 75%, more than 90% of international students graduating from back to the source of employment. With the continuous advancement of "One Belt and One Road" construction, the enrollment scale of foreign students in Gansu Province has been expanded. From 2015 to 2017, the number of foreign students enrolled in Gansu increased from 526 to 835, a growth rate of 58.7%, and the total number of foreign students in Gansu also increased by 50.5%. In 2018, Qinghai Province set up the Qinghai Provincial Government Scholarship for Foreign Students to attract foreign students to study in Qinghai. At present, more than 20 students from Turkmenistan are enrolled to study for undergraduate degree. In 2019, the number of foreign students in colleges and universities in our province has reached 291, accounting for more than half of those with degrees, among which 95 are master's and doctoral students. In 2017, nearly 12,000 international students from 156 countries and regions came to Shaanxi to study. Among them, more than 6,000 were from "One Belt and One Road" countries, accounting for 54% of the total international students in Shaanxi, which has exceeded 50% of the total international students in Shaanxi for three consecutive year (Cao, 2020; Chen & Xu, 2020; Ding, 2017; Dong & Wu, 2018; Feng, 2018; Lan, 2017; Pan, 2019; Ye, 2020; Yen, 2020; Zhang, 2017).

Significant growth in the number and scale of non-common language majors. Since the "One Belt and One Road" initiative was put forward in 2013 to February 2018, a total of 71 countries around the warzone Belt and One Readale signed "BBB1" intergovernmental cooperation agreements with China. These countries are mainly distributed in Central Asia, Southeast Asia, East Africa and Central and Eastern Europe and other regions. In 2015, the National Development and Reform Commission, the Ministry of Foreign Affairs, the Ministry of Commerce authorized by the State Council issued "the drive to build the silk road economic belt and the twenty-first century the vision and action of the Marine silk road", clearly put forward "area" initiative cooperation will focus on the "five", namely policy Unicom communication, facilities, trade flow, financing, and interlinked. To serve the national "One Belt And One Road" construction and successfully realize the "five links", the premise is to realize the language interconnection, which is both an opportunity and a challenge for the cultivation of foreign language talents in China, especially for foreign language talents who are not lingua-franca.

As of June 2019, there are 2,688 undergraduate colleges and universities (including private ones) in China (Note: the data are from the official website of the Ministry of Education), among which 532 colleges and universities offer non-lingua-franca undergraduate programs (including 135 private ones). By June 2019, the above universities will have a total of 56 non-common languages for enrollment, among which Beijing Foreign Studies University (BFSU) offers a total of 101 foreign languages, which basically cover the official languages of countries along the "One Belt and One Road" route. However, BFSU currently has only 47 non-common languages for enrollment. By the end of 2019, China's non-lingua franca undergraduate enrollment and training scale is about 54,000 people, the first language is Japanese, the annual enrollment scale is about 22,000 people, accounting for 40% of the total number of non-lingua franca enrollment. The second to eight are Russian, French, Korean, German, Spanish, Arabic and Thai with an annual enrollment of more than 1,000 students. The ninth to eleven are Portuguese, Italian and Vietnamese with an annual enrollment of more than 500 students. These 11 languages account for 94.4% of China's annual enrollment of non-lingua franca. The 12 languages with an annual enrollment scale of 100–300 students are Burmese, Indonesian, Polish, Cambodian, Czech, Hindi, Persian, Hungarian, Turkish, Urdu, Lao and Malay, which account for 3.8% of the total enrollment scale. The remaining 33 languages have a total annual enrollment scale of about 910 students, accounting for 1.8% of the total enrollment scale, and in these 33 languages, the annual enrollment is not many, basically every two or four years, some languages each enrollment is less than 10 students. The following figure shows the languages involved along the six major economic corridors of "One Belt and One Road" and the enrollment status of China's frontier provinces and cities (Cao, 2020; Chen & Xu, 2020; Ding, 2017; Dong & Wu, 2018; Feng, 2018; Lan, 2017; Pan, 2019; Ye, 2020; Yen, 2020; Zhang, 2017).

In the joint efforts of government departments and colleges concerned, remarkable achievements have been made in the construction of non-common language majors, which are characterized by the following aspects. First, with the encouragement and support of relevant national policies, the number and scale of non-common language majors in foreign languages in colleges and universities have increased significantly. According to data from March 2016, 66 non-lingua franca majors are offered in 391 specialties in 167 universities, with more than 32,000 undergraduates participating. If we add the record and approval results of undergraduate majors in 2016 released by the Ministry of Education in March 2017, the number of non-common language majors set up by Chinese universities reached 77 in 2017. These languages, together with English, French and other international common languages, have basically covered the official languages of countries that have diplomatic relations with China and the main languages of countries along the "One Belt and One Road" routes. In addition to the number of languages, the rate of increase in teaching sites is also unusual. Take 2016 as an example: according to the notice issued by the Ministry of Education, there are 63 teaching points of 34 non-common languages in 28 universities newly registered undergraduate majors. In the same year, the language with the newest teaching points is Polish, followed by Urdu, Indonesian, Persian, Turkish, etc. In addition, there are also new approved undergraduate majors, that is, 11 new languages; Second, the channels for teachers and students to go to the target language countries for further study are expanded, and the degree of international training of talents is improved. Since the 18th National Congress of the Communist Party of China (CPC), China Scholarship Council (CSC) has stepped up the training of talents in short supply, according to a press conference held by the Ministry of Education on March 1, 2017. Through international and regional issues research and high-level foreign language talent training program, 3,454 foreign language talents were sent, 1,036 of which were sent in 2016, involving 42 non-common languages and 62 countries, 32 of which were "One Belt and One Road" countries, filling in 9 domestic blank languages and cultivating a group of reserve teachers. A total of 1,207 national and regional research talents have been sent to 60 countries, 35 of which are "One Belt and One Road" countries along the Belt and Road. A group of high-quality interdisciplinary talents who understand the language and culture of these countries and the current situation of local economic development have been cultivated. Third, the compilation and publication of textbooks in non-common languages have achieved fruitful results with diversified varieties, and the application of new media and new technologies has become increasingly widespread. For example, under the leadership of the Department of Asian and African Studies of the PLA Institute of Foreign Languages, with the cooperation of Guangdong University of Foreign Studies and other universities, and with the support of World Books Guangdong, a large number of textbooks ranging from language teaching to country studies have been compiled and published. Including language introductory boutique tutorial, the first batch of state-level tutorials, the Ministry of Education characteristic specialized construction point series teaching materials, teaching achievement prizes at the national general language texts, the Chinese language undergraduate talent training base, teaching material, etc., have different levels of basic language, grammar, listening, reading, translation and other teaching materials, there are national and regional, general outline of social culture and investment environment, cultural, economic and social geography, literature, etc. Series of reader, size and the number has reached the best level in history; Fourth, the training of senior translators has been attached great importance, and the training level has achieved a breakthrough. Beijing Foreign Studies University, Beijing International Studies University, University of International Business and Economics and many other universities have successively opened the Korean translation master's degree (MTI) courses; BFSU's Master of Translation program also includes Thai. Fifth, national and regional studies have started. In 2012 the Ministry of Education approved the first batch of national and regional research breeding base in South Asia research center of Peking University, Beijing foreign studies university, such as research center of central and eastern Europe are relying on the school is the general language resources and professional advantages, focus on major national policy requirements, organization, promote the work actively, sum in research, research, service society has played a certain role, made a unique contribution to promote cultural exchanges between China and foreign countries. In 2017, more than 390 new national and regional research centers were registered by the Ministry of Education in universities across the country, of which 37 were approved at one time. A considerable part of them is concerned with non-lingua franca countries and regions, such as China Malay Research Center, Poland Research Center, Finland Research Center, Italy Research Center, etc., which already have a relatively sufficient basis for preliminary work (Cao, 2020; Chen & Xu, 2020; Ding, 2017; Dong & Wu, 2018; Feng, 2018; Lan, 2017; Pan, 2019; Ye, 2020; Yen, 2020; Zhang, 2017). From the national situation, the construction of non-common language majors has entered a new period of rearrangement and rapid development, showing overall, structural and qualitative changes.

2.2 Vocational Education

Based on 31 provinces domain the annual report on higher vocational education quality (2019) implementation of the statistics and analysis, the study found that the higher vocational education in Jiangsu international influence is obvious higher than that of other eastern coastal developed province, Hebei, Yunnan is moderately developed and less developed provinces in the higher vocational education international influence the highest province, three respectively constructed has obvious local characteristics of the new vocational education internationalization policy system.

2.2.1 Jiangsu: Building a Multilateral Multi-layer Network Coordination Policy System

The more open governance concept, the more developed vocational education system and the more solid economic foundation have jointly promoted the optimization of the policy subject, policy object, policy tool, policy content and policy evaluation of the internationalization of Jiangsu higher vocational education, forming a multilateral and multi-layer network cooperative policy system. Policy main body: government guidance, university autonomy, multinational corporation cooperation. On the one hand, the government guides rather than dominates. First, we will give full play to the guiding role of policies and publicize the combination of central and local policies. Second, adopt financial incentive means to launch a number of vocational education internationalization related plans and projects. Third, to perform the duties of referees, carry out the evaluation and project selection work. On the other hand, vocational colleges have changed from the implementer of policies to the planner, builder and participant. Jiangsu Vocational College of Economy and Trade, Jiangsu Polytechnic of Finance and Economics, Yangzhou Polytechnic of Industry, Jiangsu Maritime Polytechnic and other vocational colleges independently plan their internationalization development strategies according to their respective school conditions. At the same time, the role of multinational enterprises in the internationalization of vocational education in Jiangsu Province is more obvious. Many multinational companies, such as Zhong ding International Engineering Group, XCMG Group, Jiangsu Delong Nickel Industry Co., Ltd., German Kuka Robotics Co., Ltd., and China Post Construction Technology Co., Ltd., jointly set up overseas training and training bases with vocational colleges, set up cooperative centers and overseas branch schools, and promoted the signing of inter-school cooperation agreements at home and abroad. Policy object: to meet students' demand for high quality international vocational education public goods. Will "policy works members of society" the vocational college students as a policy object, the satisfaction of needs of a high quality international vocational education public products, committed to achieving "three changes": one is the emphasis on quantitative index to attaches great importance to the quality and quality, the second is to focus on development, focus on the growth index of three is emphasized education ability construction to serve the society contribution ability construction. Suzhou Centennial Vocational College adheres to the principle of student-oriented, respects and tolerates the cultural and customs differences of students from different countries and implements the standardized international curriculum system. Nanjing Vocational College of Tourism implements the student-centered, management, curriculum, teachers and employers five-in-one quality management system; Jiangsu Polytechnic of Finance and Economics, based on the personal wishes and interests of international students, tailors the food engineering technology and network information technology course menu, which fully meets the practical needs of agricultural development and information technology upgrading of countries along the "One Belt And One Road". Policy content: Docking international framework, implementing national policies and innovating local policies. First, we need to align international frameworks. Jiangsu Maritime Vocational and Technical College connected with the IMO STCW Convention, established the online seafarer training system of Videte Company, and jointly issued the Nanjing Declaration with the "One Belt And One Road" Seafarers Training and Cooperation Development Alliance. Five majors of Nanjing Vocational College of Tourism have passed UNWTOTED QUAL. Second, we will implement national policies. In 2018, the Department of Education of Jiangsu Province held more than ten policy information conferences, including "40 Years of Jiangsu Vocational Education Symposium", to guide vocational colleges to learn relevant national policies and regulations. Third, we will make innovations in local policies. A number of provincial relevant policy documents, used to guide local vocational colleges international work, including, Suzhou, Yangzhou, Taicang respectively introduced the municipal relevant teaching fusion, university-enterprise cooperation specific incentive measures and implementation opinions, for professional education internationalization and multinational companies go global win-win cooperation provides the system guarantee. Policy tools: Non-authoritative tools such as incentive tools and capacity-building tools play a major role. On the one hand, it attaches importance to incentive tools such as performance appraisal funds and special funds allocation to guide multinational corporations to participate in the cultivation of international technical and skilled personnel. Special policies will be issued to reward enterprise engineers to take part-time jobs in vocational colleges, encourage schools and enterprises to build training platforms for in-depth integration of industry and education, clearly stipulate the guidance of the use of special funds, allocate construction funds for the next year according to the progress and effectiveness of project construction, or encourage project construction to take pilot projects in the form of awards instead of subsidies. On the other hand, we should build a platform for international exchanges and cooperation to enhance the international capabilities of vocational colleges. Chinese and Foreign University Presidents' Forum, World Language Conference, "Jiangsu Excellent Talents for Studying Aide" Launching Meeting and "One Belt And One Road" Lysol Overseas Education Summit; We will establish th Vocational Education Cooperation Dialogue, establish a $20 + 20$ cooperation mechanism with a number of top universities in the UK, and establish cooperation alliances with the University of Ontario in Canada and the University of Macao and Portuguese-speaking Countries. Higher vocational colleges have been organized to participate in international education exhibitions in the United States, Thailand, Kazakhstan and other countries, and to hold special promotion conferences on "Studying in Jiangsu" (Ding, 2017; Feng, 2018; Yen, 2020).

2.2.2 Hebei: A "Merit-Based" Development Strategy Led by the Government

Considering the province's financial strength, the industrial development level and development of higher vocational education stage, the actual choice in Hebei "government-led" "performance evaluation" "merit" construction "special project" and other characteristics of vocational education internationalization development path, has been become a leader in the internationalization of secondary vocational education developed provinces, Hebei province. Clarify the dominant position of the government and enhance the level of internationalization with performance management. On the one hand, the government occupies a leading position in the provincial vocational education internationalization policy. First, the Education Department of Hebei Province and other relevant government departments actively organized relevant leaders of vocational colleges to study various vocational education internationalization policies formulated by the CPC Central Committee and formulated a series of provincial implementation documents. According to the policy requirements of the CPC Central Committee, it puts forward the work plan of "Learn from Germany, Raise the Level, Run the First Class" and "Ten Studies and One Promotion" in line with the situation of Hebei Province, so as to comprehensively guide the internationalization development practice of vocational education in Hebei Province. Second, we will ensure that the total amount of resources is combined with the rational allocation of resources. A number of policy documents have been issued to clearly define the minimum level of funding per student for public vocational schools, and to establish a stable growth mechanism. At the same time, according to the actual financial resources of the province, the vocational education development idea of "concentrating limited financial resources, highlighting key points, creating 'peak', striving for national first-class" has been formulated, and the construction of several well-known vocational colleges at home and abroad has been concentrated, as an important front for the internationalization of higher occupation in Hebei. The third is to carry out all kinds of evaluation work in an all-round way to realize the internal quality diagnosis and school-running optimization of higher professions. In addition, in the process of evaluation, a unified content framework and score-card should be made, and evaluation materials should be automatically generated by modern statistical analysis methods and combining with the education and teaching results of vocational colleges, thus greatly reducing the workload of evaluation in vocational colleges. On the other hand, performance evaluation provides a supervisory guarantee for the internationalization of vocational education in the province. The first is to use the results of policy evaluation to adjust policy implementation programs. Clear understanding to the vocational education in the service of "going out" enterprises in Hebei China (condition) outside the guidance, in the country (territory) outside the organization for teachers, developing countries (condition) outside of the industry or professional teaching standards for international influence indexes such as the gap, actively adjust the policy options, explore how to implement the "area" macro planning about vocational education cooperation, make joint multinational enterprises to carry out staff training, set up the overseas branch or a new model of cooperative education institutions. Second, we should implement dynamic management of important projects and their funds according to the evaluation results, strengthen supervision, guidance and performance management, establish an incentive and constraint mechanism of "top and bottom, top and bottom, top and bottom, top and bottom", adjust the construction sequence timely, and revise the resource allocation plan. Adopt the "merit-based" development strategy to build an international brand with featured projects. On the one hand, the construction of excellence has become the main strategy of Hebei vocational education internationalization policy. Facing up to the difficulties of promoting the internationalization of vocational education in Hebei Province, we will help a few projects with excellent development potential to improve their educational strength and enhance the international competitiveness of vocational education in Hebei Province through special government funding, key support and resource restructuring measures. First, in the face of industrial advantage is not obvious, strengthen educational administration. Full participation in the higher vocational education in Hebei province department of education internationalization related affairs, international exchanges and cooperation guidance education in Hebei province set up cultural association vocational education branch, ji Taiwan vocational education exchanges and cooperation, jointly sponsored BBS, with Germany's Brandenburg science, research, and the ministry of culture signed two provinces (states) education cooperation memorandum. Second, in the face of limited financial resources, concentrated power to do great things. We will standardize government revenue and expenditure activities, strengthen budgetary constraints on school-running funds, strengthen budget management and supervision, and ensure the full and effective use of funds. Under the condition that the government allocations 12,300 yuan per student for higher vocational colleges, provincial higher vocational colleges, municipal higher vocational colleges, vocational colleges run by enterprises in the industry, colleges directly under the administration of central government, and private higher vocational colleges will be supported in different proportions to maximize and effectively use the funds. Third, facing the low level of vocational education, improve the quality of education services. The overall quality of vocational education services is promoted through the cultivation of international majors and characteristic courses, the training of teachers, the construction of management systems, the establishment of scholarships and other measures. On the other hand, the key projects and characteristic projects have become the realization path of the internationalization policy goal of Hebei vocational education. First, improve the soft power of Hebei vocational education. China attaches great importance to the management of overseas students, provides more convenient conditions for overseas students to study at work, practice, social practice, entrepreneurship and other conditions, provides Chinese language teaching and a variety of cultural activities to meet the diverse needs of overseas students and improve their satisfaction with studying abroad. Second, short-term exchange and learning drive comprehensive internationalization. In addition to the number of full-time students studying abroad, the other six evaluation indexes of international influence of higher vocational colleges are among the top in China. Among them, the training amount of non-full-time overseas personnel was 392,159 person-days, 1.62 times that of Jiangsu Province with the highest vocational influence in China (241,939 person-days). The third is to pay attention to the "local internationalization" of vocational education. "Import drives export", attracting foreign teachers and students to China to drive internationalization, and alleviating international difficulties such as insufficient flow opportunities and limited capital volume. In 2018, foreign experts and teachers came to work in higher vocational colleges in Hebei province for 3,278 person days. Fourth, based on the characteristics of the major international education. Shijiazhuang Railway Vocational and Technical College, relying on architectural engineering technology, rail transportation and other characteristics of the professional, and Russia Jiao tong University jointly set up the "International Transportation School", enrollment of 400 people a year. Hebei Institute of Software Technology and many domestic and foreign units jointly build "Zu Chong College", to build a new part-time overseas training mode of "Chinese + culture + major + industry", to create an international brand of education (Cao, 2020; Chen & Xu, 2020; Ding, 2017; Dong & Wu, 2018; Feng, 2018; Lan, 2017; Pan, 2019; Ye, 2020; Yen, 2020; Zhang, 2017).

2.2.3 Yunnan: Serve the National "One Belt and One Road" Initiative

The Belt and Road Initiative is a "Chinese solution" proposed by China as an emerging power to actively participate in global governance. It is a great effort made by China to turn from an "imitator", a "learner" and an "integrator" into a "builder", a "facilitator" and even a "leader" in the global education governance system. The "Belt and Road" initiative has brought great opportunities as well as challenges to the internationalization of Yunnan higher vocational education. According to the national "One Belt and One Road" initiative layout. On the one hand, in Yunnan province in promoting the internationalization of higher vocational education, vocational education development should be brought into the party and the country to think, to plan in the overall work, positive response, tightly around the "area" initiative, with adjacent to multiple "neighborhood" all the way along the country's geographical advantages, as well as the "tea ma go" has a long history of culture origin, as, many measures actively, realize higher vocational education international influence evaluation index eight sets of data growth. In 2018, Outside in the full-time student number (more than 1 year) (1108), part-time (condition) outside personnel) (62190), student services "going out" enterprises (condition) outside practice (85653), the full-time teachers to China (condition) outside guidance and training (6584), in the country (territory) outside the organization as a post of full-time teachers (60), development and (condition) outside the professional teaching and curriculum standard (17 and 96), in the country (condition) outside skills contest number (24) compared with 2017 increased by 33.49% and 71.9 respectively 3, 234.67, 81.03, 17.65, 54.55 and

–24.41, 700.00%. The scale of overseas students in Yunnan vocational education is gradually expanding, the ability of serving multinational enterprises to "go out" is significantly enhanced, and the competitiveness of international vocational education service trade market is significantly enhanced. On the other hand, through the guidance of funds, institutional guarantee, encourage vocational colleges according to the "area" regional industrial layout adjustment, planning internationalization of vocational education development direction, relying on professional and preponderant discipline characteristic specialty, find the correspondence of education cooperation with surrounding countries, formed the service strategy "area" vocational education opening to the outside. In 2018, 13 vocational colleges in Yunnan province and countries along the "area" (Laos, Myanmar, Thailand, Vietnam, Sri Lanka, Cambodia and other 9 countries) both inside and outside the country (condition) 43 international cooperation projects, both at home and abroad for the countries along the "area" to carry out the education training 275 people, non-academic training 12219 person-time, three vocational colleges in the countries along the "area" in running schools. A total of 61 traditional Chinese cultural exchanges and training activities were held, with 1,584 people trained, laying a cultural foundation for the realization of "One Belt and One Road" and "people-to-people exchanges". Build a "One Belt and One Road" vocational education community with a shared future. On the one hand, the reform of the production and education integration ordering mode of international talent training, through the professional and industrial, school and enterprise, curriculum content and professional standards, teaching process and production process, has gradually solved the problem of deep integration of school and enterprise talent training. In 2018, Jiangsu Delong Nickel Industry Co., Ltd. and Kunming Metallurgical College jointly invested 1.6 million yuan to train 122 metallurgical materials high-skilled talents by relying on Indonesia Institute. The production and education integration ordering mode of international talent training not only realizes the complementary advantages of schools and enterprises, meets the talent needs of enterprises and achieves the win-win situation of high-quality employment, but also promotes the industrial transformation and upgrading of enterprises and the international development of vocational education, and builds a community of common destiny between vocational colleges and multinational enterprises. On the other hand, under the guidance of the "One Belt and One Road" initiative, we should improve the level of international educational exchanges and cooperation. In the Chinese culture and tourism, the tourism development in Yunnan province committee, under the guidance of Yunnan tourism vocational college to undertake for four consecutive years in Yunnan province, China—the Laotian government tourism officials and business executives communication training activities, in exploring tourism technology skilled personnel training mode of cooperation, promote the exchanges and cooperation on both sides in the field of tourism, based on the "area" initiative, the tourism exchanges and cooperation to a new stage.

Fujian agriculture and forestry university into a special fund 60 million yuan used to strengthen the "area" key areas in the cultivation of professional talents, pay attention to cultivating inter-disciplinary talent, curriculum resources and links "area", for the entire school opened 90 classes, language and culture also regularly invited expert's "area" special lectures on the guidance, make the students understanding of the "area" countries more comprehensive, three-dimensional. By cooperating with Chinese enterprises, Fujian Shipbuilding and Transportation Vocational College has made tailor-made talent training programs for local students in Africa, provided teaching resources, developed laboratory construction standards, and provided teacher training to help African countries improve the level of vocational education and lead the modernization of vocational education in Africa. Gansu province Lanzhou petrochemical vocational and technical college actively "go out", not only with the United States, Britain, Germany, Poland, New Zealand and other developed countries of the colleges and universities to establish relations of cooperation, and "neighborhood" all the way along the route of many countries such as Thailand, Brunei, Azerbaijan, Kazakhstan, and other state institutions to cooperate. On September 21, 2017, Guangdong vocational led union "area" professional education, from five countries, more than 60 of government institutions, colleges and universities and enterprises, more than 200 delegates attended the "area", led by Guangdong vocational education alliance founding conference, 54 member units to join Malaysia colleges.

Guangxi building for its own protection platform for the exchanges and cooperation between China and Asian vocational education, constantly promoting vocational education for the association of south-east Asian nations (Asian) open cooperation, establish a china-Asian vocational education and training center, China—Asian agricultural talents training center and other nine national vocational education personnel training center, for the Asian regional language, professional and technical skills in the field of agriculture, the administrative personnel more than 7000 people, entrusted organization department of the central committee of the communist youth cadre training Vietnam more than 1000 people. Guangxi Agricultural Vocational and Technical College has cooperated with Laos, Vietnam, Indonesia, Myanmar and other countries to build six demonstration bases of modern agricultural science and technology and held 68 training sessions with 1,300 trainees. Maple Leaf Vocational and Technical College Dalian has signed cooperation and exchanges with colleges and universities in Korea, Japan, New Zealand, Canada and France, and carried out student exchange programs. Dalian Automobile Vocational and Technical College cooperates with Germany and has established an education and culture company in Germany. From the introduction of simple international projects, Dalian Automobile Vocational and Technical College has transferred to the comprehensive cooperation to jointly build vocational education, exploring the unique "dual system" talent training mode, and actively building an international vocational education brand. In October 2018, Dalian Maritime Vocational and Technical College was authorized by the branch of Panama Maritime Training Service Center to train Panamanian seafarers urgently needed for the international maritime fleet. In December 2018, the Sino-German Joint Talent Training Program was established. Dalian Software Vocational College has worked closely with Edinburgh Aviation Science and Technology Co., Ltd to train high-end service talents such as flight attendants. Liaoning Light Industry Vocational College has actively carried out exchange programs with Gellar

University of Thailand, Boren University of Thailand, Hana University of South Korea and Park University of the United States. In 2017, the company established a cooperative relationship with Glauber Machine Tool (Dalian) Co., Ltd to cultivate professional talents and set up a "dual system" joint training order class (Cao, 2020; Chen & Xu, 2020; Ding, 2017; Dong & Wu, 2018; Feng, 2018; Lan, 2017; Pan, 2019; Ye, 2020; Yen, 2020; Zhang, 2017).

In 2016, Ningxia Vocational and Technical College officially launched the international student training program of China Industrial Park in Degum Special Economic Zone of the Sultan of Oman. In March 2017, the school enrolled the first batch of 38 Omani international students, who have successfully completed their studies. The second batch of 30 selected students from Oman have entered the university in September 2018. In 2017, Mingxia national vocational and technical institute and the Australian vocational education international cooperation alliance partnerships, Mingxia national vocational and technical college a year send a certain number of outstanding students take $2 + 2$ model (the first two years studying in Mingxia, after two years to study in Australia) to Australia to study, got bachelor's degree in Australia.

2.2.4 Think Tank Construction

In 2014, the Ministry of Education issued the Plan for Promoting the Construction of New Type of University Think Tanks with Chinese Characteristics, emphasizing "focusing on the urgent needs of the country and defining the main direction of attack". Public diplomacy, as a key research field of diplomacy and international issues, has become one of the main directions of the construction of university think tanks. In November 2019, the Chinese Academy of Social Sciences Evaluation (Cassese) published the Global Think Tank Evaluation Research Report (2019), which selected 20 think tanks with One Belt and One Road research characteristics, 12 of which were university think tanks. In recent years, universities and colleges have made full use of their advantages such as the concentration of talents in various disciplines, strong scientific research strength and extensive foreign exchanges. They have set up a number of think tanks devoted to the study of One Belt and One Road-related issues and actively carried out the public diplomacy of think tanks. For example, Beijing Normal University has set up a "One Belt and One Road" research institute, Beijing International Studies Universitates Belt and One Roads set up a "BBB1" strategic research institute, and Beijing Foreign Studies University has set up a Silk Road research institute. Sonya public diplomacy research institute and Beijing foreign studies university public diplomacy research center and the embassy in China, for many years, jointly organized the area "national BBS" public diplomacy, and publish the outcome "public diplomacy" area "report, focused on the" area "under the background of China's innovation concept of public diplomacy, efforts to resolve the international community to" neighborhoods questioning of the initiative and the rise of China and misunderstanding. Another example is the

Zhongyang Institute for Financial Studies of Renmin University of China, which has
hosted several international conferences on the theme of "One Belt and One Road"
and conducted practical dialogue and research cooperation with think tanks of many
countries. At the same time, experts and scholars of the think tank actively attend
international forums and conferences, and actively present the voice of a Chinese
think tank. The One Belt and One Road series of research books and reports compiled
by the think tank scholars have helped the international community better understand
the profound One Belt and One Radiation of the BBB1. At the same time, the think
tanks of colleges and universities are also building a think tank alliance, strengthening exchanges and cooperation, and making positive efforts to solve the problems
existing in the construction of "One Belt and One Road". On May 22, 2015, the "New
Silk Road University Alliance", initiated by Xi'a Jiao tong University and actively
responded by nearly 100 universities in more than 20 countries and regions, was
formally established to jointly promote exchanges and cooperation between universities and academic institutions along the "Silk Road Economic Belt" in the fields
of education, science and technology, and humanities. In the same year, the "One
Belt and One Road" university strategic alliance was established jointly by domestic
universities such as Beijing Normal University, Tongji University, Fudan University
and Tianjin University, and foreign universities such as Korea's Chongqing University and Turkish Language Research Institute, and the Dunhuang Concession was
released in Dunhuang, Gansu Province. University thinks tanks have become an
important force in the public diplomacy of "One Belt and One Road" think tanks
(Ding, 2017; Dong & Wu, 2018; Yen, 2020).

In recent years, the Gansu Provincial Government has implemented the spirit of
the Plan for Promoting the Construction of New Type of Think Tanks in Colleges
and Universities with Chinese Characteristics (2014) and the Opinions on Strengthening the Construction of New Type of Think Tanks with Chinese Characteristics
(2015) taken an active role in the construction of think tanks, establishing various
types of research think tanks. First, think tank alliances. In recent years, a number
of think tank alliances have been established, including the Tripartite Academic
Cooperation Platform of Anning Think Tank Alliance, the Think Tank Alliance of
Gansu Party School System, the Think Tank Development Research Association of
Gansu Province, and the Think Tank Alliance of Gansu Science and Technology
Innovation. Many forums and meetings have been held to promote the cooperation
among think tanks. Second, think tanks of colleges and universities. From 2010 to
the present, Gansu Province has approved the construction of 36 key research bases
of humanities and social sciences in universities. Since 2015, a large number of
new think tanks with distinctive features have been set up in universities, including
a large number of humanities research bases or think tanks. The newly built new
think tanks in universities have actively provided suggestions and suggestions for
the construction of "One Belt and One Road" and the Northwest Region/Gansu's
participation in the One Belt and One Road ruction of "BBB1" One Belt and One
Road Gansu's participation in "BBB2". Third, "One Belt and One Road" research
institutions. "One Belt and One Road" research institutes have been established in

Lanzhou University, Northwest Normal University, Northwest University for Nation-alities, Lanzhou University of Finance and Economics, and Hexi College. Taking Lanzhou University as an example, it has specially established the "One Belt and One Road" research center, with 5 national and regional research centers and 4 new think tanks of universities as the main body. In the past five years, it has approved 10 research projects, published more than 230 papers, and achieved remarkable results in decision-making consultation. The Institute of Central Asian Studies at Lanzhou University has become an important decision-making institution for the study of Central Asian issues and has been selected as the "Core Think Tank of Comprehen-sive Evaluation of Chinese Think Tanks" and the "One Belt and One Road" think tank that ranks fourth in terms of influence of university think tanks. Guangxi has set up a China Vocational Education Research Center and a think tank to conduct academic research and policy consultation on vocational education in China and ASEAN countries. In the past two years, a batch of high-quality teaching and scien-tific research achievements have been formed, and many academic monogrammers and nearly 200 academic papers have been published. These research achievements provide important theoretical references for Guangxi vocational colleges to carry out their vocational education oriented to ASEAN and serve the construction of "One Belt and One Road" (Cao, 2020; Chen & Xu, 2020; Ding, 2017; Dong & Wu, 2018; Feng, 2018; Lan, 2017; Pan, 2019; Ye, 2020; Yen, 2020; Zhang, 2017).

2.3   The Policy Issues Related to "The Belt and Road" Education

Chinese-foreign cooperation in running schools by law of the People's Republic of China the Ministry of Education supervision information platform on December 1, 2020 to update the bachelor of Chinese-foreign cooperatively-run schools and project related information to find, bachelor Chinese-foreign cooperatively-run schools and project a total of 1246, which institutions 1112, 134, the project with the coopera-tion of countries along the way "area" cooperatively-run schools and a total of 190 projects, accounting for 15% of the whole, with 65 countries along the "area" of 13 countries in cooperation in running schools, to conduct cooperation in running schools in China "in all the way along the" countries, Russia has the largest number of cooperation institutions and projects with China, while Poland and Ukraine rank second and third. From the regional distribution, China and southeast Asia, Singa-pore, Thailand, Malaysia, India in South Asia, west Asia and north Africa the United Arab Emirates, Israel, Greece, in central and eastern Poland, Bulgaria, Hungary, Ukraine and Belarus and other countries have carried out cooperation in running schools, and the five central Asian countries not to carry out the cooperation in running schools. Cooperation in running schools in our country and "area" all the way along the country agencies and projects focused on China's eastern and central parts of the western region of sporadic, Mingxia, Qinghai, Tibet, and even no cooperative education institutions and projects, the overall distribution is extremely uneven, according to former statistics about 31 provinces in China cooperation in running schools in this paper, "One Belt And One Road" cooperative education institutions and project a total of 1246, the eastern region in 688, 55% of the total, 408, the central region accounted for 33% of overall, in the western region, 150, only 12% of the whole. "Area" all the way along the country's foreign cooperative education institutions and project unit, partners almost locked in Russia, along the "One Belt and One Road" out of 65 countries, through the statistics and "neighborhoods" all the way along the 13 countries with 190 cooperative education institutions and projects, with Russia's school project, has 142, accounts for 75%, hold up half the sky "in" cooperation in running schools, cooperation object simplification.

Confucius Institutes in countries along the Belt and Road are in short supply and unscientific distribution. In terms of the number, the number of Confucius Institutes in the countries along the "One Belt and One Road" has been decreasing in recent years, and the supply obviously falls short of the demand. As a link between China and the international community, the Confucius Institute is the most basic and crucial part of the "One Belt and One Road" initiative. According to the current situation of the establishment of Confucius Institutes, among the 65 countries and regions along the "One Belt and One Road", 12 countries, accounting for 18%, have not set up Confucius Institutes. These countries also have close trade relations with China and actively participate in the One Belt and One Road ruction of "BBB1". For example, Shaaban, Adviser for Policy and Media Affairs of the General Office of Syrian President Bashar al-Assad, said at the meeting, "Syria has been a very important partner of the Silk Road since ancient times and hopes to join the 'One Belt and One Road' initiative. I believe that Syria, Iran and Iraq can build Bridges and ties." The construction of Confucius Institutes should meet the initiative of countries along the Belt and Road to participate in the construction of "One Belt and One Road", but the number of Confucius Institutes is in short supply.

From the perspective of distribution, the distribution of Confucius Institutes in countries along the "One Belt and One Road" is not scientific. Generally speaking, the larger the population of a country, the greater the demand for language learning, so more Confucius Institutes should be built. However, according to the current situation, except Russia and Thailand, the number of Confucius Institutes in other countries is less than 10, and most of them are less than 5. Nineteen countries have only one, accounting for nearly 30%. Many of these countries have a large population base and are active in international exchanges and cooperation. For example, Vietnam has a population of more than 90 million. In recent years, Vietnam has become one of China's top 10 export markets and China's largest trading partner in Asian. In view of this, only one Confucius Institute is far from meeting the needs of Chinese culture learning. It is worth noting that there are not many countries where the number of Confucius Institutes is insufficient (Cao, 2020; Chen & Xu, 2020; Ding, 2017; Dong & Wu, 2018; Feng, 2018; Lan, 2017; Pan, 2019; Ye, 2020; Yen, 2020; Zhang, 2017).

Challenges facing the education of international students. First, regional development is unbalanced. According to data on the flow of foreign students in 2018, 11 provinces and municipalities in eastern China, including Beijing, Shanghai, Tianjin, Jiangsu and Zhejiang, accounted for most of the total number of foreign students in China. In 2019, Beijing, Shanghai and Zhejiang ranked the top three in attracting overseas students. That is to say, the economic, political, cultural, social development better in the east can attract more foreign students, in the robbery students war, the eastern developed area of nature and nurture location advantages in human, taking Jiangsu province as an example, as a province of the development of foreign student's education has, in recent 10 years, the total number of colleges and universities recruit training students in Jiangsu province has been presents the fast growth momentum. This is related to the opening of "Jasmine Scholarship" in Jiangsu Province in 2010. The growth rate of overseas students in Jiangsu Province from 2010 to 2015 reached 84%.; Second, the development of the discipline is unbalanced. In terms of the subject distribution of foreign students in 2017, although the number of students who chose engineering, management, economics and agriculture increased significantly, the number of students majoring in literature still ranked first, accounting for 48.45% of the total number of students. From the perspective of Jiangsu Province, a relatively developed province in the east, "students majoring in literature have always accounted for half of the total number of foreign students in colleges and universities in Jiangsu Province, followed by students majoring in medicine, engineering, management and economics, and students majoring in philosophy, history and education have the least number". Thirdly, the structure of foreign students still needs to be optimized. From the perspective of learning types, the source places of overseas students in B&R countries are unbalanced for academic education (junior college, undergraduate, master/doctoral) and non-academic education (ordinary advanced students, advanced students, short-term overseas students). From 2013 to 2018, the majority of foreign students from Mongolia and 8 South Asian countries received academic education. The average number of Mongolian students with degrees accounted for about 70% of the total number of foreign students in Mongolia, and the average number of students with degrees from 8 South Asian countries accounted for about 87% of the total number of foreign students in China. In Southeast Asia, five countries in Central Asia and 19 countries in West Asia and North Africa, the number of foreign students receiving academic and non-academic education is relatively balanced, accounting for about 50% of the total number of foreign students in each country. In the 22 Central and Eastern European countries, the majority of international students receive non-degree education, with the number of non-degree students accounting for more than 60% of the total number of international students in the region. From the perspective of learning level, undergraduate students from countries along the Belt and Road are the majority. The proportion of undergraduate students from Mongolia, 10 countries in Southeast Asia, 8 countries in South Asia, 5 countries in Central Asia, 19 countries in West Asia and North Africa, and 22 countries in Central and Eastern Europe is between 40 and 85%. Followed by graduate students, accounting for between 17 and 56%; Junior college students are the least, the highest proportion of less than 10%. The number of non-degree students in China is mainly for general study, accounting for between 40 and 80% of the total number of non-degree students in China. It is followed by short-term study and advanced study. The number of short-term study students accounts for 19–50% of the total number of non-degree students in China, and the proportion of advanced study students is less than 5%. This shows that the proportion of post-graduate and advanced students in international students from B&R countries needs to be increased, and the education of high-level students' needs to be strengthened. From the perspective of professional demand, international students from countries along the Belt and Road mainly study Chinese. Some majors related to the "One Belt and One Road" initiative, such as information and communication, engineering technology, computer science, electronic information engineering, etc., have not received wide attention and the number of students is not large. The construction of "One Belt and One Road" is still in its initial development stage. The education of international students in countries along the Belt and Road mostly starts from Chinese teaching. With the advancement of the construction process and the increasing demand for professional talents, the number of international students studying technical majors will also increase accordingly (Cao, 2020; Chen and Xu, 2020; Ding, 2017; Dong & Wu, 2018; Feng, 2018; Lan, 2017; Pan, 2019; Ye, 2020; Yen, 2020; Zhang, 2017).

Challenges faced by the development of non-common language majors. First, language setting and enrollment scale are unreasonable. By the end of 2019, China's non-lingua franca undergraduate enrollment and training scale is about 54,000 people, the first language is Japanese, the annual enrollment scale is about 22,000 people, accounting for 40% of the total number of non-lingua franca enrollment. The second to eight are Russian, French, Korean, German, Spanish, Arabic and Thai with an annual enrollment of more than 1,000 students. The ninth to eleven are Portuguese, Italian and Vietnamese with an annual enrollment of more than 500 students. These 11 languages account for 94.4% of China's annual enrollment of non-lingua franca. The 12 languages with an annual enrollment scale of 100–300 students are Burmese, Indonesian, Polish, Cambodian, Czech, Hindi, Persian, Hungarian, Turkish, Urdu, Lao and Malay, which account for 3.8% of the total enrollment scale. The remaining 33 languages have a total annual enrollment scale of about 910 students, accounting for only 1.8% of the total enrollment scale, and in these 33 languages, the annual enrollment is not many, basically every two or four years, some languages each enrollment is not more than 10 students. The data shows that our country the general language Settings and the recruitment of student's scale is not very reasonable, too many Japanese class, supply, and some of our country "area" initiative critical languages, such as Urdu, Hindi, Turkish, Hausa, paid, from a number of colleges and universities to participate in training and recruitment of student's scale, are woefully inadequate. Hausa and Swahili-speaking, in particular, they are two of the three languages of Africa, their use is in more than 50 million population, is one of the most important language in west and East Africa, but at the moment, Hausa have undergraduate class in bewail open, only open and only four national universities have paid, other small languages every year to cultivate talents and even fewer in number. There is a shortage of teachers for these languages. After the talents trained in each session are recruited by various embassies and consulates of the Ministry of Foreign Affairs, Ministry of Culture, Xinhua News Agency, International Radio and other organizations, there are few talents left, and the annual talent output can hardly meet the market demand. The state information center "in" big data center issued the "area" big data report (2017) data show that only 2.60% of companies can provide "in the translation of" and "outside" in translation service, the enterprise all need external professional foreign language talents, common service ability is insufficient, severely restricted the Chinese enterprises to enter the local trade cooperation of countries along the "area". Second, there is a shortage of high-end professional non-lingua franca talents. In addition to the shortage in the number of non-lingua franca talents in China, there is also a structural shortage. What is needed to serve the "Belt and Road" is key high-end talents, that is, comprehensive talents who are not only proficient in the language of the target country, but also understand its national conditions, and have certain professional knowledge in international finance, economy and trade, law, etc. There are many examples of huge investment losses or even failures due to lack of research on the laws and national conditions of the investing countries. In 2010, China Overseas Engineering Co., Ltd. made a huge loss in the construction of the A2 highway in Poland. One of the reasons for the failure of the investment was that China Overseas Engineering Company did not even know that the construction of small animal passages such as frogs under the highway is a standard construction in Europe, which led to the increase of the cost and failed to adjust the price. From 2009 to 2010, CRCC won the Saudi government's EPC project contract for Mecca Light Rail, resulting in a huge loss of 4.153 billion yuan, mainly due to its lack of understanding of the Saudi market and the EPC contract and operation. In 2005, CNOOC failed to offer $18.5 billion for full ownership of Unocal, mainly because of the lack of in-depth study of the Exxon-Florio Amendment and the Energy Act of the United States. Therefore, at present, there is a shortage of comprehensive foreign language talents who not only have the background cultural knowledge of "One Belt and One Road" language, but also can engage in analysis, management and even decision-making in the international professional field (Cao, 2020; Chen & Xu, 2020; Ding, 2017; Feng, 2018; Lan, 2017; Pan, 2019; Ye, 2020; Yen, 2020; Zhang, 2017).

2.4 Countermeasures and Suggestions

Improving the system of cooperative education and optimize the layout of cooperative education. In view of the above-mentioned problems in the "Belt and Road" Sino-foreign cooperation in running schools, such as small scale of cooperation in running schools, uneven geographical distribution of cooperation in running schools, and single object of cooperation in running schools, the first is to speed up the revision of the "Regulations on Chinese-foreign Cooperation in Running Schools" and its implementation measures. With the change of internal and external environment and opening to the outside world, the Regulations on Chinese-Foreign Cooperation in Running Schools, which came into effect in 2003, has produced many inapplicable phenomena, such as the emergence of profit-making schools and the problems of running schools independently with foreign capital. In the revision, it is suggested to further expand the scope of application of the Regulations on Chinese-Foreign Cooperation in Running Schools, to bring profit-making Chinese-foreign cooperatively run schools into the normative scope, and to put forward the provisions applicable to the independent running of schools by foreign capital and the enrollment of international students. Second, we will give priority to encouraging the development of Chinese-foreign cooperatively run schools for graduate education and those with independent legal personality. In terms of the results of practice and exploration, the quality of foreign educational resources introduced by Chinese and foreign cooperative institutions is higher, the stability of cooperation and the quality of schooling are better. From the perspective of enhancing the level of cooperation in running schools, enhancing the internationalization level of higher education and expanding the international influence of China's higher education, it is suggested that the government should give priority to strengthening the development of Chinese-foreign cooperatively run schools in terms of approval, support and related policy guidance in the coming period. Third, we will support the central and western regions in developing high-quality Chinese-foreign cooperation in running schools. Future open education is a comprehensive, in view of the regional gap and short board, the state should be the financial capital support, project evaluation quota, counterpart support, admissions policies, formulate specific measures to encourage the Midwest using construction cost is low, the special advantages of the preferential tax policies, strong motivation, around the emerging and in urgent need of professional disciplines, and leap for Chinese-foreign cooperation in running schools, deciphering the Chinese-foreign cooperation in running schools regional distribution imbalance, accelerated the formation of adjust measures to local conditions, characteristics of development of education in our country opening to the outside world.

Innovating the development model of running schools and formulating the operation model by category. The construction of "One Belt and One Road" is a valuable platform for the development of international communication of Chinese language. As an important tool for communication and cooperation in the international arena, Confucius Institutes should strive to seize the opportunity of "BBB1" initiative. First, Confucius Institutes should explore the teaching mode and increase the characteristics of running schools. At the second "One Belt and One Road" Forum for International Cooperation, General Secretary Xi Jinping pointed out that "we should actively build a bridge of mutual learning between different civilizations and form a pattern of diversified and interactive people-to-people exchanges." For countries along the "One Belt And One Road", Confucius Institutes should not only be satisfied with the teaching of Chinese and culture, but also train outstanding One Belt And One Roads for the "BBB1" construction. This requires Confucius Institutes to make necessary reforms in the teaching mode, expand the teaching mode, and increase the characteristics of the school. For example, we have cooperated with foreign schools to open some diversified Chinese teaching courses, involving a wide range of professional subjects, to stimulate the interest of talents from all walks of life in the construction of "One Belt and One Road". To attract foreign students with relevant majors who have reached a certain level in Chinese culture learning to study in China and have an in-depth understanding of "One Belt and One Road" culture is not only conducive to the One Belt and One Road ruction of "BBB1" to attract talents, but also can solve the work problems of some scholars. Second, the completely unified operation mode is bound to be unable to meet the diversified needs. For Confucius Institutes, different operating mechanisms should be developed according to the specific conditions of different countries. For example, according to the policy characteristics of "One Belt and One Road", Confucius Institutes in countries along the Belt and Road should have special regulations to bone Belt and One Road serve the "BBB1" construction. In addition, countries along the Belt and Road have different ways of participating in the construction of "One Belt and One Road". In addition, due to regional and cultural differences, a completely unified law and regulations cannot meet the needs of all participating countries. Therefore, the government should take into account cultural differences, trade exchanges, policy formulation and other specific factors of various countries to formulate different operational systems in line with the actual situation. For example, in terms of teaching materials, Confucius Institutes should compile different versions of teaching materials according to local conditions. For countries along the "One Belt and One Road", teaching materials should highlight this construction focus.

Coordinating regional development and optimizing disciplinary structure. At present, the principal contradiction facing Chinese society has become that between unbalanced and inadequate development and the people's ever-growing needs for a better life. Balanced and adequate development has become the mainstream of The Times, and it is the trend of The Times. The unbalance of regional development is the result of economic, political, cultural and location factors. In the field of education for foreign students, the government can also strengthen the optimal allocation of educational resources for foreign students with the help of macro-control means, and the education structure for foreign students can be optimized through coordination, communication and cooperation in running schools among regions and universities. For example, in view of the vicious competition situation in which some colleges and universities simply attract foreign students by reducing tuition fees, reducing tuition fees and subsidizing living expenses, relevant departments can promote the rational allocation of educational resources for foreign students by raising the threshold of enrolling foreign students and strengthening the education evaluation of foreign students. At the same time, all regions and colleges should actively explore their own advantages and disadvantages in the development of education for foreign students, learn from each other and earnestly run schools, so as to occupy a place in the education market for foreign students. As far as the curriculum design of the education for international students in Chinese colleges and universities is concerned, it is difficult for some specialized courses to reflect the characteristics of the education and cultivation of Chinese overseas students. Meanwhile, some disciplines still lag behind the advanced world level in terms of the frontier and application of teaching content. To a great extent, this has affected the expansion of the scale and quality of overseas study in China. In the process of optimizing curriculum design, "localization" and "internationalization" should be fully integrated, and courses with Chinese traditional culture, folk customs and local culture should be offered to highlight the education characteristics of international students in colleges and universities. It offers international courses such as cultural comparison, comparative literature and minor languages, and provides high-quality elective courses by connecting experts and famous teachers at home and abroad, so as to enhance the international competitiveness of education for international students in Chinese colleges and universities.

Adding non-common language majors according to local conditions and cultivate multilingual and compound foreign language talents. All the way from "area" six economic corridors with frontier provinces and cities in our country the language talent training point layout, in the Russian economy, China and India economic corridor, corridor between China and Indochina, smaller economic corridor with languages set up relatively complete, each year recruitment of student's scale is not small, it is recommended that open Bengali undergraduate course school in Yunnan province colleges and universities. The frontier provinces of the New Eurasian Land Bridge Economic Corridor still lack Belarusian and Dutch undergraduate teaching sites. It is suggested that Jiangsu Province, a big province of education, set up Belarusian and Dutch in the universities with the conditions. Belarusian and Dutch are also the languages in short supply of non-common languages in China, which have broad application prospects. In the frontier provinces of China-Central Asia-West Asia Economic Corridor and even the whole country, there is a lack of undergraduate teaching sites for the common language of the five Central Asian countries. Currently, only Xi 'an International Studies University offers Kazakh major. As the frontier of the three Eurasian economic corridors in Xinjiang, non-lingua franca education should do its best along with the "One Belt And One Road" wave. At present, only 6 of Xinjiang's 54 undergraduate colleges and universities offer a second foreign language undergraduate program, and all the 6 universities offer Russian undergraduate programs, among which 2 offer Arabic. Only Xinjiang Normal University offers Urdu. It is suggested that the colleges and universities in northern Xinjiang should choose the opportunity to develop the common language of the five Central Asian countries on the basis of the Russian major. These countries used to be the republics of the Soviet Union. At present, national languages and Russian are widely used in these countries, but countries are paying more and more attention to their national languages. In addition, it is suggested that colleges and universities in northern Xinjiang should offer Persian and Turkish majors. Currently, the enrollment of these two languages is about 140 students each, and most of the teaching sites are located in the developed provinces and cities in eastern China. The supply of graduates exceeds the demand, and few of them come to Xinjiang. In the future, with the construction of the two economic corridors, Turkey and Iran will definitely carry out more and more frequent economic and trade exchanges with Xinjiang, which is located in the hinterland of Europe and Asia, and the foreign language talents trained locally will make better contributions to the economic development of Xinjiang. Kasha in southern Xinjiang is a famous city on the ancient Silk Road. It is also the starting point of the China-Pakistan Economic Corridor, an important energy and logistics artery in China. Once completed, the trade network covers the Persian Gulf region, which is of great strategic importance. At present, only Kasha University offers Russian majors, and it is suggested to add Urdu, Hindi, Arabic, Pashto and other majors. It is far from enough to only master the language skills of listening, speaking, reading and writing. It is necessary to open up our minds, innovate teaching methods, and cultivate "multiple" and "compound" talents. "Polyglot" talents refer to those who master multiple languages. They usually adopt a non-common language major, plus any general or non-common language major training mode, so that students can realize the leap from "monolingual" to "polyglot". "Compound language" talents should be trained in accordance with the national conditions of the countries along the "One Belt and One Road". For example, the five Central Asian countries now use their own national languages and Russian, and the cultivation of "multilingual" talents can adopt "Russian" + "Kazak", "Russian" + "Uzbek" and other modes. Filipino and English are used in the Philippines, and the mode of "English" + "Filipino" can be adopted. Similar to this are "English" + "Hindi", "English" + "Urdu" etc. "Compound" foreign language talents refer to those who must have certain professional ability besides language. There are usually two types of training modes: one is the education mode of monolingual major plus other professional knowledge, and the other is the education mode of non-lingua franca major plus non-foreign language and literature major. Training foreign language talents proposal arts and the sciences are action, the school of arts living to learn business, law, such as a major, and the school of science living is suggested to understand or grasp the energy, transportation, mining and other industries in a professional, because the current six economic corridors with most areas are involved in the infrastructure construction and mineral development. With the deepening of the "area" initiative, will provide the "area" all the way along the country and the world to provide broader opportunities, education as an important part of "area" initiative, will through all the way "area" initiative brings great opportunities for the development of high quality, at the same time, it will be better service "area" initiative (Cao, 2020; Chen and Xu, 2020; Ding, 2017; Dong & Wu, 2018; Feng, 2018; Lan, 2017; Pan, 2019; Ye, 2020; Yen, 2020; Zhang, 2017).

References

Cao, Y. (2020). Development status and prospects of confucius institutes under the background of "One Belt and One Road". *Modern Communication, 20*(20), 248–250.

Chen, R., & Xu, X. (2020). Research on the status quo of Gansu universities' participation in "One Belt and One Road" construction. *Journal of Northwest Adult Education Institute, 20*(1), 69–72.

Ding, C. (2017). Study on the status quo of foreign language specialization in Chinese Universities. *Foreign Language Education in China, 10*(4), 80–86.

Dong, X., & Wu, W. (2018). Research and practice on the training mode of international students in local universities. *Education and Teaching Forum, 20*(24), 11–19.

Feng, L. (2018). More than half of international students from One Belt and One Road countries in Shaanxi strengthen international cooperation and exchange in education. *Teaching and Educating People (Higher Education Forum), 2018*(33), 93.

Lan, S. (2017). "One Belt and One Road" and strategic choice of higher education development in agriculture and forestry—A case study of Fujian Agriculture and Forestry University. *China Agricultural Education, 20*(4), 7–10 + 83.

Pan, C. (2019). Thinking on Liaoning higher education internationalization and opening-up strategy. *Industry & Technology Forum, 18*(2), 210–212.

Ye, G. (2020). Qinghai education keeps making efforts in the construction of "One Belt and One Road". *Qinghai Education, 20*(04), 10–19.

Yen. (2020). Strategies for Training non-lingua-franca talents in the context of "One Belt and One Road". *Journal of Hubei Second Normal University, 37*(5), 55–60.

Zhang, G. (2017). Analysis on the education status and market development path of foreign students in One Belt and One Road Countries. *The Contemporary World, 20*(1), 74–79.

Chapter 3
Policy Analysis of the Implementation of the "One Belt and One Road" Initiative in China's Vocational Education

This chapter concentrates on examining the policy analysis of the implementation of "Belt and Road" imitative in China's vocational education. In recent years, China's higher vocational education has actively explored the path of overseas cooperation in running schools and served the construction of "One Belt and One Road". In practice, excellent cases such as Laban Workshop and Zhongshan Vocational and Technical College have been formed, and advanced experiences such as exerting industrial characteristics, participating in the construction in multiple ways and innovating the education mode have been accumulated. However, China's higher vocational colleges are still faced with various challenges from system mechanism to cooperation mode to enter the countries along the "Belt and Road", so it is still necessary to make joint efforts in various aspects to build the vocational education brand with Chinese characteristics.

3.1 Introduction

Vocational education is one of the most active field of China's foreign exchange and cooperation, in recent years, the development of higher vocational colleges has entered a new historical stage, that is, from "introduction to" primarily, to actively explore "introduced to" and "going out" the path and the mode of combining many higher vocational colleges under the "area" initiative led, the fruits of the internationalization of construction have been achieved. This article from the overseas educational practice in higher vocational colleges in our country, focusing on China's vocational education how to lead China's vocational education abroad, local service "area" initiative national strategy, and combining the academic point of view, discussions in the vocational education in our country present "area all the way along the" national education faces challenges, in order to put forward reasonable Suggestions

© The Author(s), under exclusive license to Springer Nature Singapore Pte Ltd. 2021   43
J. Li and E. Xue, *"One Belt and One Road" and China's Education Development*,
Exploring Education Policy in a Globalized World: Concepts, Contexts, and Practices,
https://doi.org/10.1007/978-981-16-3268-6_3

for the present problem, provide a reference for China's vocational education to the world.

3.1.1   The Policy Review of China's Vocational Education Service "One Belt and One Road" Initiative

In recent years, the Chinese government has issued policies related to the "One Belt and One Road" initiative of vocational education services at both the central and local levels. The contents are constantly refined. In the early stage, they mainly provide direction guidance; in the later stage, they pay attention to technical guidance at the operational level and start to pay attention to relevant incentive policies. The vast majority of higher vocational colleges have not formulated specific public policies on vocational education "going out" or school internationalization. A few colleges' official websites have related to these policies, but most of them are related to the propaganda-oriented school performance and lack policy texts. From the practice of higher vocational colleges, China's vocational education service "Belt and Road" initiative has distinct characteristics in terms of region, specialty, nature of the cooperative subject and so on (Guo, 2018; Huang et al., 2020; Li et al., 2017; Li & Zhang, 2016; Liu, 2017; Wang, 2021).

Policies of central and local governments. Since the "One Belt and One Road" initiative was put forward, the State Council, the Ministry of Education and local education departments have attached great importance to the important role of vocational education One Belt and One Ordering the "BBB1" initiative. In 2014, the State Council issued the Decision of the State Council on Accelerating the Development of Modern Vocational Education, stressing the need to stimulate the vitality of vocational schools, carry out cooperation programs between Chinese and foreign vocational schools, and explore and regulate vocational schools to run schools abroad. In the same year, a number of ministries and commissions jointly issued the Plan for the Construction of a Modern Vocational Education System (2014–2020), which required speeding up the training of technical and skilled personnel suitable for Chinese enterprises to go global. In 2015, the Ministry of Education issued the Action Plan for Innovative Development of Higher Vocational Education (2015–2018), which clearly stated that higher education should cooperate with the national "One Belt and One Road" initiative, help high-quality production capacity go global, and expand the vocational education cooperation with the count One Belt and One Road along the "BBB1". In 2016, the General Office of the CPC Central Committee issued Several Opinions on the Opening Up of Education in the New Era, which proposed to strengthen practical cooperation with other countries and multilateral organizations and give full play to the important role of education in the construction of "One Belt and One Road". In 2019, improving the "One Belt and One Road" ability of education services and expanding the opening of education to the outside world will become a major strategic task of education reform and development in the new era. "China Education Modernization 2035" takes "creating a new pattern of education opening to the outside world" as one of the strategic tasks of education modernization, proposes to comprehensively enhance the level of international exchanges and cooperation, steadily promote the "One Belt and One Road" education action, and encourage qualified vocational colleges to build "Laban Workshop" overseas. In the same year, the Ministry of Education, Ministry of Finance jointly issued by the high level on the implementation of Chinese characteristic higher vocational schools and professional opinion construction plan (hereinafter referred to as "twin plan"), the file points out: on the basis of continue to strengthen the introduction of high-quality resources, develop and launch "is given priority to with my" international standards, make China's vocational education brand, in the process of "area" and the international cooperation capacity of international technical skill training and promote cultural exchanges between China and foreign countries. In addition, according to the Higher Education Association's Guide to Overseas Running of Higher Education Institutions (Trial), the Ministry of Education will provide practical technical guidance for overseas running of higher education institutions from various aspects (Guo, 2018; Huang et al., 2020; Li et al., 2017; Li & Zhang, 2016; Liu, 2017; Wang, 2021).

On the other hand, in recent years, local governments have also introduced relevant policies to promote the "One Belt and One Road" initiative of vocational education services. Taking Beijing as an example, in 2017, the Beijing Municipal Commission of Education and the Beijing Foreign Affairs Office issued the Implementation Plan of the Beijing Education Action Plan for Connecting and Joining the "One Belt and One Road", which identified three key tasks: to carry out education cooperation; To carry out cooperation in personnel training; We will jointly build an education cooperation mechanism. In 2018, Beijing Municipal Development and Reform Commission issued the Three-Year Action Plan (2018–2020) for Beijing to Promote the Co-construction of the Belt and Road, implementing the "Belt and Road" talent training plan in the field of education, setting up national talent training fund and the "Belt and Road Scholarship" for foreign students.

From government policy, especially the central file you can see that the internationalization of China's vocational education policy in terms of connotation and focus on active service of the party and the nation's overall work, "introduction" and "going out", emphasize on the basis of the cooperation and communication, aiming at mutual benefit sharing and exchange of mutual learning, emphasize vocational education go further.

3.1.2 The Overseas Education Policy of Typical Higher Vocational Colleges "One Belt and One Road" Countries

The internationalization of higher vocational education in China presents an equal trend of "bringing in" and "going out", and the higher vocational education model with Chinese characteristics is welcomed by developing countries. According to data released by the Ministry of Education, vocational education has been opened to a higher level during the 13th Five-Year Plan period, with more than 400 vocational colleges cooperating with foreign institutions in running schools. According to the Higher Vocational Education Quality Report released annually, between 2016 and 2018, the number of teaching standards for industries or majors recognized abroad by higher vocational colleges nationwide increased from 283 to 595. Higher vocational colleges have gradually become one of the destinations for international students. The total number of international students increased from more than 7,000 in 2016 to 17,000 in 2018. Countries along the "One Belt and One Road" have become the main source of international students and the main gathering places for overseas schools. Sino-foreign cooperation in running schools continues to increase in higher vocational colleges. In 2016, more than 400 higher vocational colleges launched 923 cooperative schools and projects with foreign institutions, accounting for 42.5% of the total number of higher education institutions.

Overseas education is one of the ways for higher vocational colleges to realize internationalization. It refers to the education and training institutions set up by higher vocational colleges in China abroad with local citizens as the main target of enrollment. Compared with the overseas education activities of ordinary colleges and universities, China's higher vocational colleges and universities have shorter overseas education time, greater competition pressure, limited experience in running schools, and smaller scale of running schools. In the continuous exploration, China's higher vocational colleges and universities have formed an overseas school-running mode with Chinese characteristics.

In terms of region, China's higher vocational colleges with the highest degree of internationalization and the largest number of overseas schools are mainly concentrated in Jiangsu, Zhejiang and Shandong provinces, while the cases of overseas schools in underdeveloped inland provinces are limited. In response to the "One Belt and One Road" initiative, the cooperation in Asia and Africa has increased significantly in recent years. However, the participation of higher vocational colleges is not extensive, and the level of education is not high. From the perspective of majors, China's vocational education cooperation majors in Africa and other countries tend to focus on business, tourism service, accounting and other majors that do not require large investment, with a single discipline setting. Some majors in shortage of "One Belt and One Road" construction are involved, but the overall project introduction and specialty setting are not perfect enough.

In terms of the nature of cooperation subjects, the overseas education types of higher vocational colleges in China are mainly divided into school-school combination, school-enterprise combination and government-operation school-enterprise combination. This paper will select typical cases of various school-running modes to analyze the current policy content of "going out" in higher vocational colleges. Among them, the school-school combination of a series of "Laban Workshop" as the representative; The combination of schools and enterprises is represented by Thailand-China Rayong Polytechnic University. The combination of government administration and enterprise is represented by China-Zambia Vocational and Technical College (Guo, 2018; Huang et al., 2020; Li et al., 2017; Li & Zhang, 2016; Liu, 2017; Wang, 2021).

1. **School-school combination—Take "Laban Workshop" as an example**. In March 2016, Tianjin Bohai vocational and technical college cooperation with Thailand Ayutthaya city college, opened China to open its first overseas urban workshop, marked the Tianjin national innovation demonstration area, modern vocational education around the country all the way "area" strategy, officially launched the fruits of Tianjin excellent professional output abroad share plans with the world. At present, in the "about promoting Tianjin vocational colleges set up overseas" urban workshop "pilot program" of the relevant policy guidance, the urban workshop has proliferated in the Asian and African mainland, in Asia, Thailand, India, Indonesia, Pakistan, Cambodia, Djibouti, Africa, Nigeria, England and Portugal in Europe and other 13 countries listed, automation, new energy, railway, communications and so on more than 20 professional, set up including skills training, academic education, comprehensive coverage of secondary vocational schools, vocational education of higher vocational schools and universities and colleges of undergraduate course system of output, It has formed a brand of vocational education with Chinese characteristics and international competitiveness.

    From the point of overall orientation classmate to ban "craftsmen of the great powers" of the image as the backing, take the degree education and vocational training, a combination of vocational education and set up Tianjin dialogue and exchanges entity Bridges in the world, serving the importer of social and economic development, the internationalization of Tianjin vocational education development and the construction of teachers and professional vocational colleges.

    From the point of teaching system, Thailand urban workshop based on Tianjin vocational colleges of the construction of the internationalization of professional teaching achievement prizes at the national, "Engineering Practice Innovation Project" (EPIP) design, with Engineering (Engineering), and Practice (Practice), Innovation (Innovation), Project (Project) as the core, to incorporate theory teaching and Practice teaching is an organic whole, in actual Engineering projects, for guidance, practical application oriented, raises the student science inquisition ability and problem solving ability. The curriculum of Luban Workshop revolves around mechanization and electrical engineering, especially automation control technology and new energy technology, which are urgently needed for local development and lack of talents.

In cooperation with the teaching system, Luban Workshop shares China's high-quality vocational education resources with the world, supported by the high-quality resources of Tianjin as the national demonstration zone of modern vocational education reform and innovation. First of all, Luban Workshop has exported nearly 10 professional teaching standards and teaching resources, such as mechatronics technology, new energy technology, numerical control equipment application and maintenance, and published 16 international textbooks in Chinese, English, Thai and other languages. Together with 16 outstanding Chinese enterprises in the local settlement. At the same time, thanks to the "double-teacher" teacher system, Luban Workshop has cooperated with "One Belt and One Road" countries to carry out EPIP teacher research and training projects, which has prepared high-level teachers for the operation of Luban Workshop. Many teachers who participated in the research and training projects have become the professional backbone of the school after returning home.

In addition to teaching function, undertaking skill competition is also one of the functions of Luban Workshop. Thai city college luban workshop is the extension of our country's vocational skills contest annual venues, the related equipment technical level and international competition standards of the project, developing the international invitational tournament, friendly, conditions, urban workshop has thus become a periphery place for training and selection of outstanding technical talent, but also to promote the development of the internationalization of China's vocational skills contest.

What needs to be added is that the school-school combination of higher vocational colleges in our country is mainly seen in the cooperation with vocational education colleges in developed countries. In the countries along the "One Belt and One Road", there is less school-school cooperation in the form of school-school cooperation. In the early stage of Luban Workshop, it is necessary to encourage and promote the government's macro policies. In the later stage, there are also many excellent Chinese enterprises to join the project cooperation (Guo, 2018; Huang et al., 2020; Li et al., 2017; Li & Zhang, 2016; Liu, 2017; Wang, 2021).

2. **A combination of schools and enterprises—A case study of Thailand-China Rayong Polytechnic University**. Thailand-China Rayong Vocational and Technical University is an overseas vocational and technical university sponsored by Thailand-China Rayong Industrial Park, Wuxi Vocational and Technical College, Zhejiang Mechanical and Electrical Institute, and Zhejiang University of Economics and Trade. It offers academic education in Thailand and mainly recruits high school graduates from Thailand.

From training mode, ty the implement transnational segmentation, luo technology university joint training mode, plan recruit students 150 people a year or so, academic exchanges, 150, short-term is expected to reach about 350 students norm, the length of schooling for $1 + 2 + 1$ mode (1 year study abroad + 2 year + 1 year study abroad studying in China) or $2 + 2$ mode (2 years study abroad

+ 2 years in domestic practice), through 3-year degree recognition system to get the domestic and foreign university degree diploma. From the perspective of specialty setting, Wuxi Vocational and Technical College, Zhejiang Mechanical and Electrical College and Zhejiang University of Economics and Trade set up secondary colleges respectively according to their own professional advantages. At present, the majors of this school have been set up, including mechanical and electrical integration, computer technology and mechanical production and automation.

Compared with the school-enterprise combination, the role of enterprises is highlighted in the school-enterprise combination. Chinese enterprises in foreign countries often provide support for schools in terms of negotiation, leadership, funds and venues. On the other hand, school-enterprise combination can also make full use of educational resources to support the talent needs of enterprises, and enterprises can also solve the employment problem for the cultivated talents, so as to achieve a win-win situation for schools and enterprises. Many school-school colleges are also exploring cooperation with enterprises. For example, the newly established Luban Workshop in Djibouti was jointly built by domestic and overseas higher vocational colleges and China Civil Engineering Group Co., Ltd., realizing the transformation from "cooperation between Chinese and foreign colleges and universities" to "cooperation between Chinese and foreign colleges and enterprises".

3. **Integrating government and administration with school and enterprise— Taking China-Zambia Vocational and Technical College as an example**. China-Zambia Vocational and Technical College is the first higher vocational and technical college independently established by China's higher vocational colleges in cooperation with enterprises "going global" to carry out academic education overseas. In 2016, the Ministry of Education led the pilot work, and in August 2019, it officially opened in Luan, Zambia. "Political line between" model of combining specifically, leading the government policy support, enterprise (China nonferrous mining group) dominated the infrastructure construction, the school (Beijing industrial vocational and technical college, Nanjing institute of industry technology and so on 8 vocational colleges) dominate the connotation construction, industry, non-ferrous metal industry association is responsible for the coordination, through multiple subject to build schools, to realize optimization of running a school achievements.

From the perspective of school orientation, China-Zambia Vocational and Technical College provides skills training and academic education for employees of Chinese-funded enterprises in Zambia and the Zambian public, so as to provide strong local talent guarantee for the operation and development of Chinese-funded enterprises in Zambia, production capacity cooperation between China and Zambia and the introduction of Chinese equipment into Zambia. From the perspective of teaching design, the Zambian program has made a scientific and reasonable teaching plan and determined teaching methods suitable for Zambian students through careful research and in-depth understanding of the educational needs of schools and enterprises as well as the national conditions, people's conditions, policies, laws and educational resources of the host country.

From the perspective of training mode, the college and enterprises jointly explore the modern apprenticeship system with Chinese characteristics of "double subjects, double identities, double tutors, integration of recruitment and employment, alternating between work and study, and becoming talents in posts", to solve the Chinese communication barriers of students in the training. Graduates will also be preferred to be employed by enterprises with a salary 30% higher than the average salary. At the same time, China-Zambia Vocational and Technical College is actively exploring the teaching mode of "Chinese + vocational education" and trying to set up vocational education-oriented Confucius Classrooms to help foreign teachers and students acquire basic Chinese knowledge, Chinese usage in their professional fields, and understand Chinese history and culture. Help the employees of the enterprise to master common Chinese and cultivate local talents to communicate with each other.

Headed by Beijing industrial vocational college, moreover, a batch of higher vocational colleges are China-Zambia professional technology institute cooperative school-running mode to promote overseas to Myanmar, Kazakhstan, republic of the Congo (gold), and other countries along the "area", to point with surface, linkage development, construction of vocational education internationalization layout mode of "1 + N", explore can promote, can copy brand of vocational education with Chinese characteristics.

3.1.3 The "Going Out" Policy Characteristics of Vocational Education

It is not difficult to see from the above that China's overseas school-running exploration in countries along the "Belt and Road" is still in its infancy, with few excellent cases and no mature operational mechanism yet formed. Based on the school-running practices of several typical colleges and universities, China's vocational education "going global" mainly has the following characteristics:

1. **Respect national sovereignty and take project operation as the core**. In our country in the "area" all the way along the national vocational education aid, not the foreign aid to impose any political conditions, do not emphasize ideological and other sensitive issues, but to adhere to the "south-south cooperation", the principle of pragmatic cooperation, is committed to help countries within the range can people realize the skill level of ascension and the improvement of living conditions. The cooperation between China's higher vocational colleges and overseas colleges is also based on the negotiation and agreement signed by both sides. Usually, the project is carried out in a multi-party joint way, and the project team is formed to effectively promote the cooperation.

2. **Intensive cultivation, close to the practical needs of teaching**. In the "area" all the way along the country's school usually fit closely its development needs, in the form of smaller in concentrated some much-needed professional conduct, based on the practice of the foreign demand, and participate in the talent demand of enterprise, advocate "in middle school", in the form of the traditional small or mentoring training students and local teachers, simulate the work in the classroom, or transmitted directly through the internship practice techniques, driving the development of the local productivity.

3. **Joint construction of multiple entities and giving play to the advantages of unity**. In the exploration of running schools abroad, China's higher vocational colleges have gradually found out a school-running strategy which takes the school-enterprise combination and the school-enterprise combination of government and industry as the trend. In general, China's top vocational colleges actively explore external cooperation and become the backbone of Sino-foreign cooperation under the "One Belt and One Road" initiative. At the same time, enterprises and trade associations have solved the problems of school sites, funds, teachers and practice places for many colleges and universities. Foreign local colleges and universities are also helpful for the overall implementation of the project, so that all parties can give full play to their advantages and achieve a "win-win" situation (Guo, 2018; Huang et al., 2020; Li et al., 2017; Li & Zhang, 2016; Liu, 2017; Wang, 2021).

3.2 The Policy Experience of the "One Belt and One Road" Initiative of Overseas Education Service of Higher Vocational Colleges

The overseas running practices of the above excellent vocational colleges have laid a good foundation for the later scale expansion of China, which is embodied in six aspects, namely, the content of running a school, the subject of running a school, the mode of educating people, educational resources, educational standards and theoretical research.

3.2.1 Taking Measures According to Local Conditions and Centering on Industrial Characteristics

The different levels of industrialization development in the "One Belt and One Road" countries directly lead to the differences in their industrial product structure, international division of labor, especially in the types of international production capacity cooperation. From a practical point of view, there is great potential for countries along the "One Belt and One Road" to strengthen international cooperation on production capacity. Different regional development strategies have different demands on talents' skill quality, humanistic quality and comprehensive quality. China's higher vocational colleges can pay attention to the political and economic environment, technological development level and industrial needs of each destination country when opening overseas education, and persist in taking measures according to local conditions, focusing on local characteristic industries or urgently needed industries, and studying specific ways of running schools.

Taking "Luban Workshop" as an example, Djibouti Luban Workshop carries out training in close combination with the construction of Djibouti Free Trade Zone and talent needs of Djibouti Railway Project. Indonesia Luban Workshop serves local economic development by focusing on automobile maintenance, intelligent manufacturing and new energy technology; Thailand Luban Workshop has set up two majors, namely (high-speed railway) EMU Maintenance Technology and (high-speed railway) Railway Signal Automatic Control, to focus on the construction of Thailand's high-speed railway. The professional education network of high-speed railway covers the whole country of Thailand and Southeast Asia, and continues to train professional technical and technical talents for Thailand and Southeast Asian countries. Luban Workshop in India focuses on intelligent manufacturing and new energy technology; Pakistan Luban Workshop to carry out energy and electricity cooperation; The UK Luban Workshop sets up the middle-class cuisine specialty by relying on the characteristic specialties of the two universities. Each of them has its own strengths, and the specialty positioning is highly consistent with the economic development of Tianjin.

On the other hand, colleges and universities also make full use of their own geographical advantages when offering vocational education overseas. Vocational college of land and resources in Yunnan province based on "China facing southeast Asia, South Asia talent training base" mineral resources advantages, industry and mining the doe, Laos and Cambodia industry bureau of geology and mining of hand signed a joint agreement mineral resources, talent cultivation, and Laos institute to build joint training center for students in vocational skills training. The person in charge of Hainan Vocational College of Economics and Trade introduced that the school made full use of the international tourism island and favorable geographical advantages in "One Belt and One Road", and established cooperation channels with many universities in Russia, Belarus, Kazakhstan, the United Arab Emirates and Pakistan. Nanning Polytechnic has built a modern vocational education development center in Guangxi and Hong Kong to carry out vocational education courses, qualification certification, skill competitions and international exchanges and cooperation for the central and southern China, southwest China and Southeast Asian countries.

3.2.2 Participation of Multiple Subjects, Integration of Industry and Education, and Attention to Enterprise Needs

With the progress of China's "going out" strategy, Chinese enterprises in overseas' employment difficult problems also increasingly, walk out of enterprises lack the necessary local talent support, a batch of higher vocational colleges has used the practical experience proved that multivariate main body participation, the integration is to build high quality production and education vocational education one of the most effective path of opening up to the platform. Government involvement provides support at the policy level; As the main body of participation, the school focuses on the connotation construction of colleges and universities. Industry participation helps coordinate resources; The participation of enterprises provides demand orientation, training content and learning standards for overseas vocational schools. In turn, vocational education itself provides high-quality talents and technical and intellectual resources for enterprises.

Take China-Zambia Vocational and Technical College as an example, the needs of enterprises have determined the orientation of running school for the college. Before the establishment of the school, the Zambia project went through the process of domestic communication and investigation of the working group in the early stage, field investigation of the working group in the middle stage, and collective investigation of the operation and production equipment of the enterprise by all the teachers in the later stage. Through understanding the needs of the enterprise, the teaching plan and program were formulated. Second, the needs of enterprises determine the training content of vocational colleges. Through the investigation, the college found that the current problems of employees are mainly language communication barriers and skills deficiencies. For this reason, the project team finally selected several types of flotation operators, electricians, instrument workers and hydraulic bench workers as the first phase of the training program. Meanwhile, students are required to pass the CET6 before they can obtain the graduation certificate. Thirdly, according to the needs of the enterprise, the project team has formulated a complete set of code of conduct and operation specifications for the students, which on the one hand helps the enterprise to improve production efficiency, on the other hand, it also ensures the standard of teaching and production process. Fourthly, vocational education itself provides technical guidance and intellectual support for enterprises, and directly selects and sends teachers to conduct guidance in enterprises. At the same time, the workshop as the classroom environment, teaching enterprise staff to overhaul equipment, troubleshooting. Finally, the vocational education in many "One Belt and One Road" countries is still in the stage of book theory and lack of practice. The emergence of enterprises provides a practice base for local vocational education and greatly improves the training quality of high-skilled talents (Guo, 2018; Huang et al., 2020; Li et al., 2017; Li & Zhang, 2016; Liu, 2017; Wang, 2021).

3.2.3   Innovate Education Mode, Highlight Characteristics, and Build Brand

In the past, China's vocational education abroad mainly consisted of teacher dispatching, short-term exchange and other projects, without in-depth exploration of education mode. After the exploration of several higher vocational colleges, higher vocational colleges continue to innovate education mode in running overseas, highlight the characteristics of colleges, and try to build a brand of Chinese vocational education.

First of all, Luban Workshop, China-Zambia Vocational and Technical College and other institutions provide "vocational training + academic education", which on the one hand teaches students knowledge and skills, and on the other hand meets the needs of students from the host countries, especially employees of enterprises, to obtain higher education. Secondly, higher vocational colleges going global flexibly use the "online + offline" dual platforms to realize resource sharing among multiple learning points through Internet technology, develop high-quality classroom resources such as micro-courses, and overcome the limitations of space and time. Third, represented by tai Luo vocational and technical college in many university-enterprise cooperation overseas educational mode implements "local + China" double region school-running mode, offer certain quota of foreign students a year, to accept the host country students coming to China to study Chinese technology and culture, at the same time local management personnel and technical backbone to accept ability training stage in China, multi-angle, multi-channel cultivation enterprise need talent.

In addition, our country's higher vocational colleges are exploring the possibilities of innovation education, such as in vocational and technical college to carry out the "vocational education + Chinese" Confucius classroom Chinese teaching mode, which are characterized by vocational education, vocational training, to enterprise staff, industry as the main task of Chinese teaching Chinese language and culture, in addition to arrange travel management and other professional teachers and students to share knowledge of Chinese history and culture, cultural experience activity, school teaching attaches great importance to the spread of Chinese culture at the same time, to deepen the exchanges with the outside world, built a bridge for the hearts and minds are interlinked.

3.2.4   Education Resources Go Out Synchronously to Achieve Sustainable Development

In order to realize the sustainable development of educational aid, only aid equipment and funds are far from enough. The overseas education mode of higher vocational colleges in China insists on simultaneously going out with teachers and teaching materials, so as to achieve the real "teaching people to fish". By teachers to go out, is not only meant to send teachers to go abroad, but in "speaker + ta" teaching mode, with the way for the study of hiring foreign teachers to participate in teacher training, on the one hand can more fully, prepares a lesson in detail, on the other hand can give full play to the role of the excellent teachers, promote the other teachers grow, on this basis, the praise in vocational college and other institutions also explore "teacher + students" and "teacher + enterprise technical personnel", outstanding students in the learning process and the enterprise staff training to become teachers with teaching ability, for colleges and universities reserve faculty, promote the independent development of colleges and universities. In addition to teachers, teaching materials, courses and other teaching resources are also conducive to the sustainable development of vocational education in China. For example, Luban Workshop, as mentioned above, provides learning resources such as micro-class and virtual class through online platform to help students overcome the obstacles of time and region. Another example is the North Engineering Branch of China Zan Vocational and Technical College, which sets more than ten curriculum standards and develops bilingual textbooks, and Luban Workshop publishes multilingual learning textbooks (Guo, 2018; Huang et al., 2020; Li et al., 2017; Li & Zhang, 2016; Liu, 2017; Wang, 2021).

3.2.5 Actively Promoting Chinese Standards

Higher vocational education's "going global" also drives Chinese standards to "go global" simultaneously. Higher vocational colleges with the combination of schools and enterprises have promoted the internationalization of Chinese curriculum standards and industry standards in the process of running overseas. In vocational and technical college as an example, Beijing industrial vocational and technical college to lead independent research and development of automation and information technology professional standards, and adopted the Zambia official recognition, become China's first enter the sovereign national professional standards of national education system, cooperation in the field of surveying and mapping, construction and other mechanical and electrical, complete curriculum standard and paradigm, and contributed to the internationalization of the Chinese curriculum standard. In the same project, Guangdong Vocational and Technical College of Construction compiled a series of industrial standard documents, such as the professional standards for scaffolders in the non-ferrous industry, which were applied to the operation of enterprises and trainee training in Zambia to standardize the operation of trainees, improve the working level of trainees and expand the international influence of China's industrial standards.

3.2.6 Regularly Summarizing Experience and Attach Importance to Theoretical Research

Walk out of China's vocational education experience is insufficient, Luban workshop and other representative institutions in grope for overseas education attaches great importance to the experience summary and theoretical research at the same time, set up "the area along the college research center", established by the higher vocational colleges, teaching and research institute of vocational education center, professional team, the subject research around the school construction, and all kinds of research centers were set up branch in domestic and abroad research on vocational education cooperation mechanism, to jointly develop international education standard, and provides consultation for school construction, advertising and other services.

3.3 The Current Challenges Faced by the "One Belt and One Road" Initiative of China's Vocational Education Service

Faced with the policy guidance of the country and the need of school construction, many higher vocational colleges are urgently seeking or improving their overseas education in the countries along the "One Belt and One Road". At the same time, after several years of exploration, the typical vocational colleges mentioned above are also faced with a series of problems such as teachers, venues, systems and mutual recognition of achievements, which can be summarized into five aspects: top-level design, cooperation connotation, qualification framework and law, brand building and theoretical support.

3.3.1 In Terms of Top-Level Design, There Is a Lack of Unified Planning, and the Educational System Environment Is Not Perfect

Although in vocational and technical college, workshop and so on in practice has made certain achievements, but overall, the higher vocational colleges in our country in the "area" all the way along the country's overseas education limited, basic autonomous exploration stage, the lack of policy planning in the design of the top support, school system environment is not sound, the bilateral cooperation mechanism is not clear. The education department has no clear guidance for the assessment of internationalization of vocational colleges, insufficient incentive measures, absence of encouraging policies, and imperfect laws and regulations. According to the dean of the Vocational College of China and Zambia, although the eight schools actively participated in the pilot project, their participation was not consistent due to the different policies of different provinces and cities. For example, some schools found it difficult to send teachers due to the lack of indicators for going abroad. It can be seen that the coordination between government departments and policies is not in place, and the implementation of policies is difficult. In terms of funds, China has not yet established a financial support system, and many institutions' funds and equipment are provided by cooperative enterprises and institutions of both sides as well as social donations. There are large gaps in start-up funds and aid funds. In the later stage, the scale expansion, model promotion, equipment maintenance and other aspects of the college are faced with funding difficulties. In addition, the normative mechanism of school-enterprise cooperation has not been established, there is a lack of win-win profit distribution mechanism for enterprises' participation, there is often poor communication between colleges and enterprises, and colleges cannot meet the production and operation demands of enterprises (Guo, 2018; Huang et al., 2020; Li et al., 2017; Li & Zhang, 2016; Liu, 2017; Wang, 2021).

3.3.2 In Terms of Cooperation Mechanisms, the Connotation and Ways of Cooperation Need to Be Deepened

China's higher vocational colleges along with the number of countries cooperation in running schools although increased, but the overall cooperation still exist such problems as small scale, single channel of communication, many vocational colleges lack of understanding of the educational significance of "going out", the overall planning of education internationalization and the ability to mobilize resources, the vocational education services all the way "area" strategic thinking is insufficient, especially the interior node cities, the internationalization of vocational colleges are marginalized, trivializes situated status, realize their own advantages, the enterprise needs, combining the successful save few in overseas markets.

From the perspective of the connotation of cooperation, the current higher vocational colleges in China have insufficient understanding of the connotation of overseas education. School management and local education departments have a one-side understanding of internationalization as the introduction of excellent foreign experts or experience, short-term exchange and training, etc. On the one hand, vocational education teachers do not have the foreign language teaching ability; on the other hand, they lack the understanding of international vocational education standards, teaching methods, curriculum models, etc., and the overall international teaching level is weak. From the perspective of cooperation mode, the vocational education cooperation between China and other countries along the Belt and Road is mostly carried out by means of student exchange, teacher exchange, skill training, etc., which fails to reach a general consensus on the substantive and in-depth level, which is not conducive to vocational education playing its due role in the construction of service "One Belt and One Road".

From cooperation platform, at present, a lot of building international cooperation platform is the official nature, industry, enterprises and other related main body participation enthusiasm is relatively low, participate in the cooperation of vocational colleges also has strong regional features, and in vocational education development strategy planning, policy making and development of personnel training mode of substantive areas has not yet reached broad consensus, vocational education service ability of multilateral economic and social development also needs to be further improved, lead to an omni-directional, multi-type and long-term mutual benefit cooperation network system in a wide range of areas.

3.3.3 In the Process of Cooperation, There Is a Lack of Regional Qualification Framework and Local Laws Are Not Applicable

The cooperation in vocational education cannot be separated from the conversion between vocational and non-vocational education and between academic qualifications and non-academic qualifications in different countries. This conversion standard is usually stipulated by the national qualification framework, for example, the EU and other member states have interconnected national qualification frameworks, which facilitate the transnational flow of education and talents. However, China has yet to establish a national qualification framework, a lack of standards for the transition between vocational qualifications, academic qualifications and learning outcomes, and a certification system for its cooperation in vocational education with other regional countries, which hinders cross-border learning and work. Another big obstacle in running a school is mastering the laws of other countries. Host can without violation of international agreements in accordance with the law of foreign investor education service of subject qualification, the proportion of total investment and to a certain limit, want to establish a mutual recognition of professional qualification and academic degree system also needs to have enough knowledge of other countries' law, that higher vocational colleges by domestic individual effort is also very difficult to achieve (Guo, 2018; Huang et al., 2020; Li et al., 2017; Li & Zhang, 2016; Liu, 2017; Wang, 2021).

3.3.4 Lack of Unified Standards for Brand Building

According to the empirical research of Chinese scholars, Ruban building institutions such as the large demand for college construction standards, represented by the Ruban press China vocational education brand in the selection of partner schools enterprises, set the internationalization of professional courses, international local internationalized talents cultivation, the teachers lack of unified standard, high quality teaching resources, is not conducive to long-term operation and sustainable development of relevant brand colleges and universities. On the other hand, as the "Confucius Institute" of vocational education in China, the problems of "Luban Workshop" in brand building are manifested as the lack of condensed core spirit of talent cultivation, and the concepts of "Ban Mo Culture" and "Great Country Craftsmen" have not been refined and effectively propagated, so there is still room for improvement in brand building.

3.3.5 Lack of Theoretical Support and Research Support

For vocational education to go abroad and take root and sprout in societies with different cultural backgrounds, it cannot be separated from the guidance of theoretical research to practice. Once the overseas colleges and universities are completed, theoretical research is needed to support the realization of the expected results of the projects, the expansion of the scale and the replication of the project experience. On vocational education in our country at present abroad study are limited, most is about the "area" initiative under the background of vocational education opportunities and challenges, the minority is about some outstanding case of experience introduction, at the reading of literature, the colleges and universities to carry out the results of empirical study only one, and not enough in-depth, at the same time, because time is short, small, relatively dispersed and other objective reasons, related research as a whole is still in its infancy. The lack of research results on the vocational education or economic and labor structure of the countries along the "One Belt and One Road" route, the implementation results of excellent cases of vocational education in China, the coordination of various elements of overseas vocational education, etc., cannot provide operational guidance for other vocational colleges eager to carry out international co-housing.

The optimization path of the "One Belt and One Road" initiative of vocational education service. Throughout a typical practice of overseas education in higher vocational colleges and the vast majority of higher vocational colleges face the plight of China's vocational education to realize effective, long-term, sustainable service "area" initiative, also need to be pointed at the top-level design, connotation, communication mechanism, the qualifications and standards system, a breakthrough brand construction and theory research.

Improve the top-level design and improve the laws and regulations related to the "going global" of vocational education. At present, most overseas vocational education in China is in the stage of independent exploration. In order to serve the construction of "One Belt and One Road" well, it is necessary to perfect the domestic layout, judge the development space, make a good development plan and form strategic coordination. The government should take vocational education as an important link in the construction of "One Belt and One Road" at the level of top-level design, refer to China's Higher Education Overseas School Guide and other policies in the field of higher education, and formulate a detailed and perfect system guarantee.

To improve the construction of relevant laws and regulations, we should pay special attention to the following points: First, we should form a policy guidance to encourage vocational education to "go global", form a platform between government and enterprise schools, and provide certain financial guarantee and resource support; Second, encourage enterprises to actively participate in the overseas running of vocational colleges, regulate enterprises' participation in relevant projects in terms of laws and regulations, and clarify the profit distribution rules between enterprises and colleges; Third, according to the types and characteristics of vocational colleges running overseas, relevant guidance and suggestions should be issued to provide policies and certain intellectual support.

Based on excellent cases, deepen international exchanges with multiple subjects. At present, the communication mechanism among schools, governments, industries and enterprises at home and abroad is not perfect enough, especially the cooperation involving enterprise participation is mostly led by the government. In this aspect, the government should take the initiative to build a platform between government, school, industry and enterprises, so as to promote the participation of multiple subjects in vocational education to go out. At the same time, the majority of higher vocational colleges should fully realize the strategic significance of the "One Belt and One Road" initiative of vocational education service, actively learn advanced experience in running schools, seek complementary advantages among different subjects, and deepen the connotation of external cooperation and international construction. Higher vocational colleges that have gone abroad should also pay attention to the summary and extraction of experience, share experience in running schools and resources, and deepen cooperation in majors and teachers, so as to "go abroad" together and improve the overall quality of internationalization of education.

Improve the multi-platform communication mechanism, improve the mutual recognition of qualifications, and actively participate in the formulation of standards. In the face of the lack of communication channels, higher vocational colleges through domestic foreign enterprises, provincial inter-ministerial and schools such as communication and coordination, set up the China international education conference, world vocational education colleges and universities alliance, "area" collaborative education league, China association of south-east Asian nations (Asian) vocational education "double hundred" flagship program, the vocational education cooperation between China and Asian nations alliance platform, such as, at the same time, make good use of all kinds of folk combination and nonprofit organization support, personnel training, consulting services and quality certification, to promote higher vocational international cooperation, promote international exchanges and cooperation in higher vocational ability in an all-round way. At the same time, national education authorities also need to communicate with other countries in a timely manner to improve mutual recognition of vocational qualifications, academic qualifications and learning outcomes, so that talents from both sides can flow freely and efficiently. With vocational education in our country and superior enterprises

go abroad, vocational colleges also needs to realize the importance of active participation in international standards, combined with China post qualification, teaching
resources and "neighborhoods" all the way along the country's education system,
widely absorbs domestic and international professional standards, the establishment
conforms to the international advanced professional course system and standard of
professional standards.

**Combine standardization with specialty construction to create a brand of
vocational education with Chinese characteristics**. The current overseas education exploration of higher vocational colleges fully reflects the characteristics of
colleges and industrial enterprises. However, there are more features and less norms.
Compared with Germany's "dual system" and Australia's TAFE institute, there are
still very few international brands of high-quality vocational education with Chinese
characteristics. In this regard, Chinese vocational education brands such as Luban
Workshop should establish standardized and standardized models as soon as possible,
based on current practice, follow the internal logic of development, and realize
standardized procedures of access, operation and development. Admission criteria
include conditions of cooperative institutions, construction objectives, construction
plans, expected results, etc. Operation standards include teaching resources, international teaching, teaching mode, teacher training, talent cultivation, etc. Development
objectives include routine standardization system, quality evaluation and supervision system, equipment management, performance appraisal, internship system, etc.
The characterization construction level, in addition to the professional advantages,
combined with colleges itself workshop and so on should also strengthen brand
positioning, brand image and cultural construction, mining on the basis of class ink
cultural spirit power, with the organic combination of modern science and technology
of China, improve local students' interest in China and cultural identity, as "area"
strategy can help build a bridge of culture (Guo, 2018; Huang et al., 2020; Li et al.,
2017; Li & Zhang, 2016; Liu, 2017; Wang, 2021).

With the help of the "One Belt and One Road" strategy, the construction of
China's vocational education brand can also fully absorb the advanced experience of
other countries and solve the problem of its own vocational and technical personnel
training. There are many countries along the "One Belt and One Road" with large
scale and high-quality vocational education, such as Russia, Singapore, Israel and so
on. Deepening the cooperation with the governments and institutions of these countries and improving the mutual recognition of academic credentials and exchange
of study abroad systems are also conducive to improving the quality and system
of China's domestic vocational education, supporting the "going out" of vocational
education and establishing a vocational education brand with Chinese characteristics.

**Strengthen theoretical research to support policy formulation and implemen-
tation**. As stated earlier, Ruban workshop and other advanced vocational colleges
has been cooperation with scientific research institutions, government agencies, such
as set up their own research center, to summarize the practical experience and the
deepening of the research cooperation mechanism, on the academic level, however,
the current academic research should focus on seeking innovation on research topics

and research methods, to make more achievement of the research is more conducive to the practice in higher vocational colleges.

On research topics, research should be attention ought to be "more transferred to it from the reality, a thorough investigation into the" area "all the way around the historical conditions, economic structure, labor demand, education structure, investment in China, establishing the national archives for the vocational education, in the service of vocational colleges" going out plan formulation; In addition to introducing the excellent overseas cases of higher vocational colleges in China, it can also focus on the experience of developed countries in carrying out educational assistance in relevant countries, so as to provide reference value for China's vocational education assistance. We can also focus on the cases or models that are not successful enough to reflect on the reasons for their failure. On the research methods, should be integrated use of quantitative and qualitative analysis, case studies and other research methods, multi-level and multi-field, multi-dimension and multi-angle research on vocational education internationalization, strive to comprehensive and in-depth specifying external cooperation in higher vocational colleges in China are faced with the problem and the existing experience, for China's vocational education brand to provide a solid operational reference value towards the world (Guo, 2018; Huang et al., 2020; Li et al., 2017; Li & Zhang, 2016; Liu, 2017; Wang, 2021).

References

Guo, J. (2018). Action strategies for internationalization of vocational education from the perspective of "One Belt and One Road": Analysis based on policy framework and practice model. *Education and Occupation, 20*(5), 28–34.

Huang, Y., Deng, W., & Chen, W. (2020). The motivation and path of China-ASEAN vocational education cooperation under the background of "One Belt and One Road" construction. *Education Science, 36*(04), 83–89.

Li, Y., Yang, Y., Rui, F., Yang, R., & Yu, L. (2017). "Luban Workshop"—The new fulcrum of the international development of vocational education. *China Vocational and Technical Education, 20*(1), 47–50.

Li, Z., & Zhang, P. (2016). The innovation of internationalization development of Tianjin vocational education in Bohai "Luban Workshop". *China Vocational and Technical Education, 20*(16), 11–19.

Liu, H. (2017). Development Characteristics and trend of higher vocational education in China in 2016—Publication of 2017 annual report on quality of higher vocational education in China. *China Vocational and Technical Education, 17*(22), 5–9.

Wang, L. (2021). Research on the overseas running path of higher vocational colleges in china under the background of "One Belt and One Road"—A case study of joint biding for overseas universities. *Occupational Technology, 20*(1), 1–7.

Chapter 4
The Policy Analysis of the Higher Education for "One Belt and One Road" Initiatives Implementation

This chapter concentrates on exploring the policy analysis of higher education for "One Belt and One Road" imitative implementation. We provide intellectual support to the Belt and Road Initiative and establish an alliance of think tanks for research in countries along the Belt and Road. Build a "One Belt and One Road" resource and element sharing platform to promote multicultural communication. At the same time, the B&R countries are faced with the following challenges: diversified education systems, lack of experience in trans-regional cooperation in higher education, and insufficient supply of policy support; Cultural differences among countries along the Belt and Road are great, and there is an imbalance between the supply and demand of high-level personnel training. The promotion of bilateral and multilateral cooperation mechanisms of multi-parties needs to be strengthened. Different and diversified practice modes of higher education cooperation are insufficient, and the communication and cooperation ideas are limited. The level of higher education cooperation needs to be improved. The cross-border cooperation guarantee system for higher education is not sound, and the quality of cooperation needs to be improved. The implementation of higher education service "One Belt and One Road" initiative should improve the top-level design policy system, focus on the interaction and coordination mechanism of higher education, and improve the project certification standard system. Adhere to cultivate people by virtue, through the higher education service "One Belt and One Road" initiative major field action plan, the development of high-level international national talent training mode; For universities, it is necessary to strengthen the internal and external cooperation and improve the international cooperation system construction of the "Belt and Road" higher education.

© The Author(s), under exclusive license to Springer Nature Singapore Pte Ltd. 2021
J. Li and E. Xue, *"One Belt and One Road" and China's Education Development*,
Exploring Education Policy in a Globalized World: Concepts, Contexts, and Practices,
https://doi.org/10.1007/978-981-16-3268-6_4

4.1   Introduction

Xi jinxing general secretary in 2013 during a visit to Kazakhstan and Indonesia, successively put forward to build economic belt "silk road" and "Marine silk road" in the twenty-first century "area" initiative, in 2016 the Ministry of Education issued "promote to build" area "education campaign", emphasized the education mission and made education action plan. In Beijing in August 2018, xi jinxing, chairman of promoting the construction of "area" chaired a working 5 anniversary of the symposium, put forward the "area" construction from the overall planning of the "spring" into "collaborate-style painting" intensive cultivation, to high quality development, countries along the benefit of the people, promote to build community of human destiny; In 2019, the Central Committee of the Communist Party of China and the State Council launched the "Modernization of China's Education 2035". This is the development stage of "One Belt and One Road" initiative. Education plays a fundamental and guiding role in the One Belt and One Road of "BBB1". Educational exchange and cooperation are One Belt and One Road the important content of "BBB2" construction, but also the key One Belt and One Road that determine the success or failure of "BBB3" construction. Higher education service "One Belt and One Road" advocates the coexistence of opportunities and challenges under the guidance of national One Belt and One Road strategy. "BBB1" advocates the internationalization and modernization of higher education, which conforms to the demands of The Times for the construction of a strong country in higher education and "Double First-Class". Therefore, this paper, taking 42 double first-class universities in our country service "area" initiative to implement policies and measures as the research object, combing the main content and features, analysis of policy implementation of systems and mechanisms, research to improve higher education service "area" initiative to implement institutional guarantee and pattern construction, all the way to "neighborhoods" policy perfect, theoretical research and construction forward to make a beneficial attempt (Cui & Song, 2019; Gu, 2015; Liu & Zhang, 2020; Min, 2019; Yang, 2018).

4.2   Policy Content and Implementation of Higher Education Service "One Belt and One Road" Initiative

Chinese universities serve One Belt and One Road mainly by providing educational support and cultivating talents for relevant countries. At the same time, they also actively promote the exchange of young people in the join One Belt and One Road development of BBB1 countries. During the 13th Five-Year Plan period, in-depth international cooperation between universities has been carried out extensively. More universities are actively building high-level international science and technology cooperation platforms, participating in international big science programs, serving the "One Belt and One Road" initiative, and going abroad to deeply participate in global science and technology governance. We will encourage institutions of higher learning to carry out high-level research cooperation with high-level foreign universities and research institutions in superior disciplines and technological fields.

(1) **Strengthen "One Belt and One Road" international talent training, establish a high-level education cooperation alliance and jointly create a degree program**. According to the Ministry of Education, by the end of April 2019, China had signed agreements on mutual recognition of higher education degrees with 24 "One Belt and One Road" countries, and 60 universities were operating overseas in 23 countries along the Belt and Road.

In May 2019, in order to enhance international talent training and serve the construction of "One Belt and One Road", Peking University launched the International Undergraduate Program to One Belt and One Road of the "BBB1" talent training and "Future Leaders" international double degree undergraduate program. "Future Leaders" International Dual Degree Undergraduate Program is a degree program jointly created by Guanghua School of Management, Peking University, and world-renowned universities to build a high-level education cooperation alliance. It aims to cultivate international talents who are "rooted in China, connected with the world, based on The Times and facing the future". Guanghua School of Management has established cooperation with 14 universities from 13 countries and regions, including Moscow State University, York University in Canada, National University of Singapore, Tel Aviv University in Israel, and will select outstanding young talents from the cooperative universities. After completing the first two years of undergraduate study in their home country or region, students return to Peking University for another two years. In terms of curriculum, PKU and its partner universities will jointly develop some characteristic courses, such as courses on China's development and Chinese culture, and invite experts in various fields to give lectures, so that students can have a deeper understanding of China. Students from top international business schools and students from Peking University will spend two years at Peking University's "One Belt and One Road" College, where they will build a sincere friendship, cultivate a multicultural vision, open and inclusive spirit and critical thinking, understand China and the world deeply, and embrace the new era of globalization.

With the promotion of the "One Belt and One Road" initiative, international exchanges and cooperation among Chinese universities have become increasingly frequent and in-depth, and the number of One Belt and One Road from "BBB1" countries studying in China has continued to increase. According to the Ministry of Education, there were 492,200 students from 196 countries and regions studying in China in 2018, of which 260,600 were from countries along the "One Belt and One Road" routes, accounting for 52.95 percent of the total (Cui & Song, 2019; Gu, 2015; Liu & Zhang, 2020; Min, 2019; Yang, 2018).

(2) **Establish a special organization of "One Belt and One Road" to inno-vate the cooperative school system.** In April 2018, Renmin University of China (RUC) announced the establishment of the Silk Road College, which is a non-independent legal entity affiliated with RUC and located at the RUC Suzhou campus. At the beginning of its establishment, the Institute will offer the "Contemporary China Studies" program, which mainly enrolls master's degree students from "One Belt and One Road" countries and regions along the Belt and Road. The length of study is 2 years, and the research direction is divided into Chinese politics, Chinese economy, Chinese law and Chinese culture, all of which will award master's degree in law. In the future, the school will explore related projects with other schools in the university. Silk Road College students enjoy full scholarship, including tuition, accommodation, medical insurance and other expenses for international students. At the end of May 2019, the "Belt and Road Initiative for University Partnering between China and the UK" was officially launched in Beijing. The initiative aims to strengthen multilateral cooperation between universities of China, the UK and countries along the Belt and Road. British Lancaster university in June 2019 was formally established in the "area" research institute, Lancaster university has been involved in a series of related to "neighborhoods" all the way of cooperation and communication project, looking forward to the new guiding function to the institute to become "area" of "area" research base, to provide valuable advice to relevant government, also look forward to institute as china-UK cooperation platform, for china-UK relations "golden age" of output more "golden fruit". Xinjiang has undertaken most of the tasks of education coop-eration with Central Asia at the national level, and established bilateral and multilateral cooperation, exchange and coordination mechanisms. Colleges and universities in Xinjiang have set up 10 Confucius Institutes in Russia, Kyrgyzstan, Kazakhstan, Pakistan and other countries, and more than 20,000 overseas students are studying in these institutions. Facing central Asia to make the area along the "education core, during the period of" much starker choices-and graver consequences-in, to further expand international education exchange and cooperation strategy in Xinxiang, to strengthen college through developing central Asian studies, a form of innovation, promote a shortage of professional and in colleges and universities around the region's key disci-plines for Chinese-foreign cooperation in running schools, and increase finan-cial support for international promotion of Chinese central Asia base (Cui & Song, 2019; Gu, 2015; Liu & Zhang, 2020; Min, 2019; Yang, 2018). Xinjiang will further expand the scale of relevant seminars, favor government officials, think tank scholars and enterprise elites from countries along the Silk Road Economic Belt in terms of training targets, and support universities in estab-lishing Central Asian cultural studies and Confucius Classrooms, so as to grad-ually lay a solid foundation for conducting practical exchanges and cooperation with Central Asian countries. Fifty-one universities from China, Central Asia and seven countries along the Silk Road Economic Belt have established the "China-Central Asia University Alliance" in Urumqi, aiming to build an open

and international interactive platform. With the help of this platform, in the future, China and Central Asian countries will gradually carry out student exchange, credit mutual recognition and other joint training projects, provide a number of preferential policies for exchange students, issue academic certificates of both sides, so as to promote complementary advantages and substantial cooperation in running schools, and cultivate "One Belt and One Road" international talents.

(3) **Deepen "One Belt and One Road" scientific and technological development services and innovate the scientific and technological cooperation mechanism along the Belt and Road**. Since its establishment in 2016, the "One Belt and One Road" scientific and technological innovation alliance has been building a "science and technology community" featuring equality, mutual benefit and win-win cooperation through effective cooperation mechanisms since its establishment three years ago. Alliance with the "area" countries to build joint laboratories, joint training talents, invited along the national outstanding scientists working in China, set up advanced applicable technology, management and policy of science and technology training, positive for the "area" of countries and regions along the development of science and technology service, exploring the road to a win-win science and technology innovation cooperation. One Belt and One Road has 26 members from 12 countries.

Shanghai Jiao Tong University and the Moscow Aeronautical Institute are both members of the "One Belt and One Road" scientific and technological innovation alliance. The two sides have established a joint research institute, carried out the cooperation of bachelor's and master's double degree programs, and will gradually establish a joint research center. The SJTU Bulgarian Center, which was established in 2016, has also signed cooperation agreements with a number of Bulgarian universities and academic institutions, and set up a branch center at the University of Sofia. Relying on the Shanghai "Belt and Road" Young Scholars Program, the Research Center for Nanoscience and Technology of Shanghai University has carried out in-depth cooperation with the National Center for Nanotechnology of Thailand. Shanghai University has also worked closely with the State Technical University of Belarus to jointly build a platform for the incubation and transformation of scientific and technological achievements between Chinese and Belarusian universities, focusing on strengthening cooperation with science and technology industrial parks, financial capital and key enterprises in the industry, effectively promoting the transfer and transformation of excellent scientific and technological achievements in each other's countries. CAS Shanghai Branch has built a collaborative innovation platform, established a long-term cooperation mechanism, and carried out international cooperation plans in key fields such as biomedicine, energy, environment and materials in the Belt and Road countries, which have achieved remarkable results (Cui & Song, 2019; Gu, 2015; Liu & Zhang, 2020; Min, 2019; Yang, 2018). Since the "One Belt and One Road" initiative was put forward, Shaanxi Angling and Northwest A&F University have extended their agricultural research achievements to relevant countries and One Belt and One Road along the "BBB1" and helped them develop agriculture with "Chinese solutions". With the "One Belt and One Road" initiative deeply rooted in the hearts of the people, more countries are seeking agricultural cooperation with China. In 2016, Northwest A&F University initiated and established the "Silk Road Agricultural Education Science and Technology Innovation Alliance", which now has 76 universities and research institutes from 14 countries and regions.

At the 23rd China Angling Agricultural High-tech Achievement Expo in 2019, various and colorful international exchange activities broke through the geographical restrictions and set up a new bridge for international agricultural cooperation and exchange. During the meeting, under the sponsorship of the northwest agriculture and forestry university of science and technology, China, Russia, Kazakhstan, Jordan, 12 countries such as Poland and 23 36 universities research institutions, jointly established during agriculture high education of agriculture science and technology innovation alliance "silk road", will be held on a regular basis education of agriculture science and technology cooperation BBS "silk road". Northwest A&F University plays an important role in the agricultural cooperation of "One Belt and One Road" countries. Relying on the relevant policies of Angling "China Agricultural Science City", industrial advantages and its own scientific research strength, the university has carried out extensive cooperation with countries along the "One Belt and One Road" in agricultural industry, agricultural science and technology and culture exchanges, talent joint training and other fields. Founded in 2015, the "One Belt and One Road" Research Think Tank Alliance of Belt and Road Countries is jointly initiated by 17 domestic universities and research institutions. It brings together experts and scholars in different fields of politics, economy, culture and other fields to make innovative exploration for the joint construction and sharing of resources, information and achievements. In the past six years, Chinese think tanks have combined their professional strengths and disciplinary advantages, constructed relevant evaluation index system and launched a series of blue books, which has become an important way to help the construction of "One Belt and One Road". Russia's eastern central Asia research institute, Chinese Academy of Social Sciences "in" the Chinese Academy of Social Sciences research center of the "in" the blue book: "One Belt And One Road" construction development report, Shanghai academy of social sciences, the "area" all the way along the research on China's strategic pivot layout with the urban network, Beijing second foreign languages institute of China academy of "area" strategy "blue book" in "China investment security, etc., are all the way" area construction provides intellectual support (Cui & Song, 2019; Gu, 2015; Liu & Zhang, 2020; Min, 2019; Yang, 2018). As an international university, Beijing International Studies University (BISU) has built a unique university think tank. On the basis of clarifying the three research directions of "One Belt and One Road" investment security, language strategy and cultural exchange, we will conduct in-depth research on the countries and regions along the "One Belt and One Road" by relying on the advantages formed over a long period of time and provide think tank products One Belt And One Reedsport the "BBB1" to go deeper and deeper. In October 2015, 47 universities from 8 countries along the "One Belt and One Road" established the "Belt and Road"

University Strategic Alliance One Belt and One Road build the "BBB1" higher education community. With the advancement of "One Belt and One Road" strategy, the demand for political, economic and cultural talents from countries along the Silk Road is increasingly strong. The shortage of talents and low degree of sharing of educational resources have become the constraints in the One Belt and One Road construction of "BBB1".

In order to promote the cooperation between universities along the Belt and Road in the fields of education, science and technology, culture and other fields, Lanzhou University, Fudan University, Luhansk State University of Ukraine, Chongqing University of South Korea, Kuala Lumpur Jian she University of Malaysia and other 47 universities have joined the "One Belt and One Road" university strategic alliance. In addition to building a platform for sharing academic resources, the alliance will also explore the exchange mechanism between researchers and students, establish a collaborative innovation community, jointly carry out research, jointly cultivate talents with an international perspective, and serve the economic and social development of countries and regions along the "One Belt and One Road". Lanzhou University of Finance and Economics and Belarusian State University are preparing to establish a China-Belarus International Finance Research Office, which will provide theoretical guidance for Gansu Province to establish a China-Belarus Industrial Park in Belarus. Chinese universities serve the Belt and Road Initiative, mainly by providing educational support and cultivating talents for relevant countries. At the same time, they also actively promote the exchange of young professional and technical talents in the joint construction of "One Belt and One Road" countries. He cited the establishment of the Tsinghua University Southeast Asia Center in Bali, Indonesia, in 2018 to train local engineers and other technical personnel to adapt to future industrial development. In addition, Tsinghua University has also set up the China-Africa Leadership Development Center, International Engineering Education Center and other institutions to strengthen cooperation with other countries.

4.3 The Higher Education Service "One Belt and One Road" Initiative Implementation Policy Issues

The "One Belt and One Road" initiative is a new concept, model and strategy of global governance put forward by China based on both international and domestic situations. Ready-made experience and model can guide, at the same time, "One Belt And One Road" connected along the northeast Asia, central Asia, southeast Asia, South Asia, west Asia, north Africa, central and eastern Europe and other regions of 65 countries, different national conditions, cultural and historical background and different economic and social education development, social system and economic model diversity, interests are diverse, in the "area" under the background of national strategy, cross-border regional education both in the management system, innovating the mode of cooperation mechanism and build a perfect system security is faced with many challenges.

(1) **Countries along the Belt and Road have diversified education systems, lack of experience in carrying out cross-regional cooperation in higher education, and lack of policy support**. First of all, the differences in education systems in the countries along the Belt and Road lead to obstacles in academic and degree certification. "Neighborhood" all the way along the national and regional economic development level, and the development level of different education foundation, different countries education system, also including along the national language diversity, this is the "area" education cooperation training talents in the process of mutual recognition, mutual recognition of credits, and brings great challenge to academic degree qualifications authentication, etc.

Secondly, the lack of experience in cross-regional educational cooperation leads to the lagging supply of educational policies. Since the reform and opening up, our country in more than 40 years. In the process of education opening up, we have accumulated some experience and gradually explored a development path with Chinese characteristics. However, education cooperation mainly focuses on student flow, cross-border cooperation in running schools, international school construction and international education assistance. In education cooperation of countries along the "area" all the way to lead the sex, the dominant role, coordinated each participation main body, the omni-directional plan as a whole higher education cooperation target, innovation cross-regional education mode of cooperation, build a cross-regional formation and matching belt education cooperation organization and education cooperation mechanism is very necessary, due to lack of experience of policy supply, ideas to build and support resources lags behind, is undoubtedly a huge challenge for our country.

Thirdly, the foreign exchange management level of colleges and universities is not high, and the second-level colleges are insufficient. In terms of foreign exchange management, the management level lags behind the development of disciplines, and there is a mismatch between the management level and the development level of disciplines. Most secondary colleges do not set functional institutions or professional staff for foreign exchange and cooperation. The division of power and responsibility between administrative functional departments and teaching units in secondary colleges is not clear enough, and there are overlapping functions and repeated management. All departments lack of organic cooperation and assistance, the relationship is not close enough, and the work efficiency is low. The foreign exchange work of some colleges and universities is mainly guaranteed by administrative compulsory requirements. They lack the self-conscious research ability and endogenous motivation, the overall plan for carrying out foreign exchange and cooperation, the clear goal of running a school, the way to achieve it and the system guarantee, and the effective cooperation and coordination of various department (Cui & Song, 2019; Gu, 2015; Liu & Zhang, 2020; Min, 2019; Yang, 2018).

Finally, the quality assurance system of higher education cooperation in "One Belt and One Road" countries is insufficient. In our country and the developed countries must accelerate the domestic education qualifications framework, realize the education quality guarantee system, student and teacher flow system, bilateral and multilateral cross-border education mechanism, the regional higher education qualifications framework, gradually realize the "area" integration of regional higher education as well as the qualification of the job market and employment standards of the integration of China Unicom and docking. In the absence of mature conditions for higher education cooperation, the basic and leading functions of higher education in "One Belt and One Road" cooperation cannot be brought into play.

(2) Cultural differences among countries along the Belt and Road are large, the supply and demand of high-level personnel training is unbalanced, and the promoting force of bilateral and multilateral cooperation mechanisms with multi-parties needs to be strengthened. In 2016, the Ministry of Education issued the Education Action to Promote the Joint Construction of the "Belt and Road", which provided policy support and implementation plan for comprehensively promoting the "One Belt and One Road" construction in the field of education. The One Belt and One Road initiative is a systematic project of the century.

It only marks the new beginning of China's national development strategy and diplomatic strategy, but also brings new challenges and opportunities for China's education reform and development. With the continuous expansion and deepening of education cooperation between China and the countries along the "Belt and Road", new requirements and challenges have been put forward to the construction of trans-regional higher education cooperation mechanism. The consultation and coordination mechanism of higher education in "One Belt and One Road" countries is hindered by cultural differences. Education consultation and coordination mechanism is the "area" all the way across different regions during the process of regional cooperation and coordination between the national strategy, an important part of the policies, rules, mainly related to education and the "area" of the construction of the political and economic coordination, education overall strategy will coordinate with national, regional, colleges and universities, cross-regional cooperation education quality and the cooperation and coordination, etc. We need to strengthen cross-border people-to-people and cultural interaction mechanisms, education policy dialogue mechanisms, education cooperation and consultation mechanisms, and emergency management mechanisms. We need to enhance international understanding education and country studies among B&R countries, and support education think tanks in B&R countries to conduct joint research and jointly hold forums. In particular, we should draw on the coordination and consultation capabilities of cross-border organizations along the Belt and Road such as the Shanghai Cooperation Organization, the East Asia Summit and the

Asia-Pacific Economic Cooperation, and build on the impetus of existing bilateral and multilateral cooperation mechanisms such as the China-Arab States Cooperation Forum and the China-Mongolia-Russia Economic Corridor to promote the formation of new cooperation mechanisms among countries along the Belt and Road. Socio-cultural differences in countries along the routes impede cross-border movement of people. Cultural differences are one of the major challenges faced by the countries along the "One Belt and One Road" in carrying out trans-regional educational cooperation. Since China's reform and opening up, China's foreign exchange and cooperation of center of gravity is mainly concentrated in the European and American countries and regions, for the "area" all the way along the route covered by central Asia, west Asia, north Africa, central and eastern Europe countries relatively few cultural cognition, language, religion, values and other aspects of the cultural differences will no doubt about the future of education cooperation, particularly cross-border communication between teachers and students constitute obstacles and risks. Especially in the aspect of religion, only 28.6% of the 65 countries along the "Belt and Road" have the same official religion, and the majority of countries along the "Belt and Road" have a high degree of religious concentration, prominent religious differences will form an important cultural risk. Moreover, the education of international students presents the tendency of the integration of traditional effectiveness and the mission of the new era; The imbalance between supply and demand of high-level talents training of both international level and national attributes is prominent. There is a significant gap between the realistic demand and the objective supply of vocational education (Cui & Song, 2019; Gu, 2015; Liu & Zhang, 2020; Min, 2019; Yang, 2018).

(3)   Difference and diversity of higher education cooperation practice model innovation is insufficient, exchange and cooperation ideas are limited, and the level of higher education cooperation needs to be improved. First, the uneven educational level of countries along the Belt and Road hinders educational cooperation. "Neighborhood" all the way along the country's major covers the northeast Asia, southeast Asia, South Asia, north Africa, central Asia, central and eastern Europe and other regions of the country, on the whole, level of education development, especially the development of higher education level is relatively lags behind, the education development scale, development level and education quality is uneven, this will be the future of cross-regional education cooperation mechanism construction to bring serious challenges. It is urgent for higher education cooperation to pay attention to the national conditions of different regions and even different countries in the same region, adopt differentiated policies and develop diversified practice models.

Secondly, for a long time, in terms of foreign exchanges, higher education exchanges and cooperation have been in a single way, with narrow majors, which makes it difficult to achieve short-term breakthroughs and leads to insufficient collaborative innovation in higher education. "One Belt and One Road" puts forward a new mission for the foreign exchange and cooperation of China's higher education—running schools abroad. Colleges and universities can independently set up overseas branch schools and establish cross-border university alliances with foreign universities. At the same time, a new form of "One Belt and One Road" integration of industry, education, research and application has gradually taken shape. There is a huge gap of international talents, which provides an unprecedented opportunity for Chinese universities and enterprises to cooperate in cross-border development. Exchanges and cooperation in domestic colleges and universities are limited to academic conferences, scholar visits, student exchanges, joint training of graduate students, etc. However, these exchange activities are usually not deep enough and of low level due to the lack of standardized management and incentives. There are some deficiencies in building overseas campuses, carrying out scientific research cooperation, participating in overseas construction projects, and introducing foreign experts and teachers. In the projects and activities that have been carried out continuously, teachers are still based on visits and inspections, with a small audience and few participants. The level and strength of higher education cannot be reflected in professional lectures and mutual recognition of degrees. Take China University of Mining and Technology for example, the students from countries along the Belt and Road are mainly at the undergraduate and master level. Among them, the majority of postgraduate students cannot adapt to the school's teaching environment well and cannot keep up with the normal teaching process. In addition, the non-degree overseas students in CUT are mainly ordinary advanced students and short-term exchange students, and only a few advanced students.

Thirdly, with the rapid development of economic globalization, the internationalization of higher education is also developing towards a new situation. Various elements and resources begin to flow spontaneously around the world to form the highest allocation of "cost performance". China's higher education as a whole, however, subject construction on the whole, there are unbalanced development, ecological problems such as unreasonable, embodied in the construction of teacher's team, quality of personnel training, scientific research platform and the symbolic achievements, internationalization and so on four aspects, which to some extent, limits the "area" of higher education international cooperation model of innovation.

(4)   **The cross-border cooperation guarantee system of higher education is not perfect, and the cooperation quality needs to be improved**. As mentioned above, the international political situation is complex, ethnic cultural differences are significant, religious infiltration and interference, the degree of cooperation is uneven, the common vision of cooperation is different, etc. At the same time, the foreign student education in our country is faced with "unreasonable structure of students, lacking the ability to talent training, social support environment is not mature, the safety pressure inadequate response to the" strict challenge, such as "One Belt And One Road" along the line of the developing countries along the foreign student education level is low, foreign students in the developed countries of small scale, "output - input" imbalance

between country and area "quality, efficiency" significant difference. Therefore, in the construction of higher education service "One Belt and One Road", international students' education shows the tendency of combining the traditional effectiveness with the mission of the new era. The imbalance between supply and demand of high-level talents training of both international level and national attributes is prominent. There is a significant gap between the realistic demand and the objective supply of vocational education.

The foreign exchange and cooperation management system, resource guarantee system and monitoring and evaluation system of Chinese colleges and universities are not perfect, and the cooperation quality is not guaranteed. In the management system of colleges and universities, the International Cooperation and Exchange Department and the International School are respectively established under the promotion of education internationalization. The International Cooperation and Exchange Department is mainly responsible for administrative affairs such as Hong Kong, Macao and Taiwan affairs, international platforms, international projects, Confucius Institutes and overseas alumni. The International School is mainly responsible for the language teaching and life management of the students jointly trained by the international students and the university. The course management of international students is mainly in the charge of the second-level college of their major. There is no professional staff in each college to manage international students, and the poor communication between international students and the college leads to many difficulties in course selection and examination for international students. Meanwhile, teachers of various majors do not have high requirements for and pay insufficient attention to international students, which leads to a very high failure rate for international students. In addition to the management of international students, the second-level college should also fully cooperate in scientific research to help the university achieve high-level foreign exchange and cooperation. Because only by relying on the college to hold academic exchange activities and international exchanges can we truly penetrate into the teachers and students, so that the important role of international exchange and cooperation can be given full play. If the school's foreign exchange and cooperation are separated from teachers and students, it will not be able to promote the smooth development of international foreign exchange work, nor will it be difficult to achieve substantive breakthroughs and progress. The promotion of foreign exchange and cooperation is usually led by the International Exchange Office or the International School. There is no clear division of the functional scope of the department's foreign exchange and cooperation, which leads to the problem of improper allocation of resources or poor coordination. As a result, it is difficult for the university to get the understanding and support from teachers of other colleges in the process of promoting foreign exchange and cooperation, and finally, the operation is not smooth and rigid in terms of teaching and teachers. The "One Belt and One Road" cooperative management system and the lack of professional management personnel limit the quality improvement of foreign exchanges and cooperative activities (Cui & Song, 2019; Gu, 2015; Liu & Zhang, 2020; Min, 2019; Yang, 2018).

Finally, due to the lack of quality assurance and supervision mechanism in the cross-border education market, the tracking and monitoring system, information feedback mechanism, quality evaluation and incentive system of cross-border coop- eration in higher education, as well as the risk avoidance and dispute settlement mechanism of cross-regional cooperation cannot be smooth. Should actively build "area" in the higher education community cooperation more perfect risk aversion mechanism and dispute settlement system, actively signing bilateral and multilateral education cooperation framework agreement, international conventions, to develop education cooperation through the system construction, dredge and optimizing step by step along the countries because of the policy environment, the education system and the cooperation and communication bottleneck caused by cultural differences, the power of higher education service "area" initiative of the construction of the quality assurance system (Cui & Song, 2019; Gu, 2015; Liu & Zhang, 2020; Min, 2019; Yang, 2018).

4.4 Policy Suggestions for the Implementation of Higher Education Service "One Belt and One Road" Initiative

Over the past six years, our country's higher education services "area" initiative to implement cooperation framework is built, then, to the overall strategy of the "neigh- borhoods" policy system framework, and innovation "to consolidate and strengthen One Belt And One Road" initiative system, mechanism and mode of cooperation, the innovation of higher education service system of "area" initiative to implement security system, to achieve "area" of higher education cooperation areas and scope expands unceasingly, standardization of binding.

(1) **Improve the top-level design policy system, build a network of think tanks for international cooperation in higher education, and set up special plan- ning teams to make overall planning**. "One Belt and One Road" cross- regional education cooperation strategy should adhere to the guidance and responsibility of China's education policy planning and governance. To build a "One Belt and One Road" higher education zone led by China, assisted by various countries and promoted by various parties. To strengthen inter- governmental cooperation and test the opening up of education under the new situation, it will be a unique cross-border higher education cooperation zone in the world spanning three continents and covering 65 or more countries. We will gradually build a "One Belt and One Road" think tank with higher education characteristics, establish a trans-regional think tank cooperation network for higher education, carry out policy research on cross-border coop- eration and opening-up of higher education, and provide suggestions for higher education to serve the implementation of the Belt and Road Initiative. After a thorough investigation, on the basis of the government and related education department should set up specialized planning group, the overall design "area"

all the way across the framework of regional education cooperation mechanism system and construction paths, clear key task for the construction of mechanism, the concrete implementation plan, schedule and roadmap, and set up a consultative committee, Suggestions and comments on the major problems in the process of implementation.

Against the "area" all the way across the region education cooperation mechanism construction experience insufficient supply of education policy lag problem, higher education is an urgent need to establish service "area" initiative implementation of form a complete set of quality guarantee system, including the area along the "higher education district funds supporting system for the support and assistance, and degree of regional credit system of mutual recognition of degree, diploma qualifications framework and recognition system and area employment standard system, etc.

(2)   **Focus on the interaction and coordination mechanism of higher education, improve the certification standard system of projects, and enhance the quality of exchanges and cooperation**. All the way "for" area social cultural differences lead to the cross-border flow of countries along the barrier, should actively promote the hearts and minds of countries along the same construction, education and international understanding "area" fate community building, promote the citizens of countries along the cultural identity and education identity for each other, thus reducing turnover. We will establish research bases in B&R countries and regions, conduct cooperative research with B&R countries in the fields of politics, economy, culture and ethnic groups, and integrate education for international understanding, cross-cultural understanding and Silk Road cultural heritage into the process of cross-border education cooperation and the curriculum system of primary and secondary schools in B&R countries (Cui & Song, 2019; Gu, 2015; Liu & Zhang, 2020; Min, 2019; Yang, 2018).

References

Cui, C., & Song, Y. (2019). Cultivating intercultural talents in colleges and universities to help "One Belt and One Road" construction. *People's Forum, 30*(21), 133–135.

Gu, M. (2015). "One Belt and One Road" and the mission of comparative education. *Comparative Education Research, 57*(6), 1–3.

Liu, B., & Zhang, H. (2020). Research on cross-regional educational cooperation mechanism from the perspective of "One Belt and One Road". *Fudan Education Forum, 18*(5), 86–92.

Min, Y. (2019). Research on Foreign exchange and cooperation of universities under the background of "One Belt and One Road". *China University of Mining and Technology, 20*(12), 13–19.

Yang, J. (2018). The opportunities and challenges of "One Belt and One Road" to higher education in China. *Education and Teaching Forum, 20*(1), 213–214.

Chapter 5
Policy Analysis of "One Belt and One Road" Initiatives in China's Basic Education System

This chapter involves examining the policy analysis of "One Belt and One Road" initiatives in China's basic education system. The One Belt and One Road, as a new development background, is an important historical development opportunity for China. Since the One Belt and One Road was implemented, China and neighboring countries have achieved mutual benefits. The development of One Belt and One Road is inseparable from talents, and education is the main way to train people. Therefore, the One Belt and One Road cannot develop without education, and education also obtains a new chance under the One Belt And One Road development. On the one hand the number of students coming to China to continue to increase, on the other hand, China's education also gradually go abroad, basic education as the basis of the entire education work plays a foundation role, at present our country foundation education opening to the outside world expands unceasingly, there are some excellent primary and secondary schools abroad, overseas schools, spread the culture of education and educational experience, but at present the policy is not enough complete, will not be able to motivate some excellent schools abroad, so we need to complete the related policy, continue to push forward the process of basic education opening to the outside world.

5.1 Development of Basic Education Under the Background of One Belt and One Road

5.1.1 One Belt and One Road Educational Background

"One Belt and One Road" is a transnational strategic cooperation concept based on economic and trade as the main carrier, with connectivity as the core concept and mutual benefit as the basic purpose. It is an inheritance and promotion of the

J. Li and E. Xue, *"One Belt and One Road" and China's Education Development*,
Exploring Education Policy in a Globalized World: Concepts, Contexts, and Practices,
https://doi.org/10.1007/978-981-16-3268-6_5

ancient Silk Road. Its Asia-pacific economic circle in the east to the west European economic circle, along the way connected to central Asia, southeast Asia, South Asia, west Asia and East Africa in 64 countries, is an open, inclusive, Pratt & Whitney economic cooperation initiative, unlimited range of country, is not an entity, no sealing mechanism, the will of the countries and economies are involved, common development, cooperation and development. "One Belt and One Road" strategy has broken the original point-like, block-like regional development mode, and become a new development mode. Most of the countries along the "One Belt and One Road" are emerging economies and developing countries, with a total population of about 4.4 billion and an economic aggregate of about US$21 trillion, accounting for 63% and 29% of the global total respectively. These countries are generally in a period of rising economic development, with different resource endowments and strong economic complementarities. There is great potential and space for cooperation between them. If you are poor, you will be free from poverty, and if you are good, you will help the world. This has been China's responsibility to the world since ancient times. Today, as China is about to build a moderately prosperous society in an all-round way and step into the ranks of moderately developed countries, the launch of the "One Belt and One Road" strategy and the establishment of the Asian Infrastructure Investment Bank reflect this sentiment. Education bears a unique mission in promoting the construction of "One Belt and One Road" (Li & Duan, 2019; Song & Liu, 2019; Sun, 2009; Wang & Wang, 2016; Zhou, 2017).

During his visits to Central and Southeast Asian countries in September and October 2013, Chinese President Xi Jinping put forward the major initiatives of jointly building the Silk Road Economic Belt and the 21st Century Maritime Silk Road (One Belt and One Road). "Area" initiative is profound changes, the party central committee and the State Council according to the global situation as a whole of the international and domestic two overall situation to make important strategic decisions, to establish a new system of the open economy, form features each other aid, sea and land as a whole new pattern of all-round opening to the outside world, to achieve "two one hundred" goal of realizing the great rejuvenation of the Chinese nation the Chinese dream, promote the development of world prosperity and peace and stability, has important and far-reaching significance. The "One Belt and One Road" strategy involves not only hard power such as infrastructure construction, trade and investment and industrial cooperation, but also soft power such as policy, culture and talent. In a sense, soft power plays far better than hard power. Talents are the fulcrum and key of "One Belt and One Road" construction. The success or failure of education is related to the success or failure of talents, and further related to the success or failure of "One Belt and One Road" construction, and the development of education and talents lies in scientific planning. The "One Belt and One Road" strategy not only tests the talent training in China over the past 30 years, but also provides valuable opportunities for the reform and opening up of the next round of education. Mr. Gu Ming yuan, a senior educationist in China, also pointed out that although "One Belt and One Road" takes economic cooperation as the core, economic development inevitably involves technological cooperation and cultural exchange, which is the key and education is the foundation. Both affirm the importance of education in the context of One Belt And One Road development. Meanwhile, Shanghai ranked first in the PISA test in 2009 and 2012 respectively. The quality of China's basic education has been recognized by the world. Shanghai Century Publishing Group signed an agreement with HarperCollins Publishing Group to translate and publish mathematics textbooks for basic education in Shanghai at the opening of the London Book Fair in 2017. It is the first time that a complete set of curriculum materials from China has been included in the UK basic education curriculum system. China's basic education can go out, also should go out and we all have been in introducing foreign educational mode and idea, now our country's basic education has made remarkable achievements, which greatly increased the confidence of our culture, so our basic education needs to go abroad in order to China's experience to provide a basic education in the world (Li & Duan, 2019; Song & Liu, 2019; Sun, 2009; Wang & Wang, 2016; Zhou, 2017).

5.1.2 Basic Education Under the Background of One Belt and One Road

On July 13, 2016, the Education Action to Promote the Joint Construction of "One Belt and One Road" issued by the Ministry of Education clearly pointed out that Chinese education will consistently adhere to opening up to the outside world and build a "One Belt and One Road" education community on the basis of equality, inclusiveness, mutual benefit and win-win, so as to fully support the joint One Belt and One Road construction of "BBB1". Education plays a pivotal role in the joint construction of the Belt and Road Initiative, playing a fundamental and pioneering role. The opening up of education to the outside world is comprehensive, including not only higher education, vocational education, but also basic education. But the discussion has mostly focused on higher and vocational education, with little reference to basic education. As a matter of fact, basic education, as the foundation of the whole education system, plays a very important role in the "One Belt and One Road" strategy and has a great potential. Looking back at history, we seem to see such scenes: during the height of the Tang Dynasty, Japan, Vietnam, Korea and many countries in Central Asia and West Asia sent thousands of noble children to study in Tang and study together with Chinese children. Today, more than 1000 years later, with the help of "One Belt and One Road", China's basic education seems to be once again presenting a splendid scene of educational and cultural exchanges between China and foreign countries. China's education, especially basic education, has obvious advantages of solid foundation and high quality. "One Belt and One Road" has opened up a new path for the internationalization of China's basic education and created a more favorable environment for China's basic education to open up and run schools and go abroad. To consciously participate in the "One Belt and One Road" common development of the grand strategy. Efforts should be made to rely on the geographical advantages of "One Belt and One Road" along the land and coastal areas, and actively participate in the "Action to Promote the Joint One Belt And One Road of" BBB1 "Education". With people-to-people exchanges as the way, mutual understanding among the people as the core, mutual learning among civilizations as the means and the development of human civilization as the goal, we should enable children of different countries, different colors and different cultures to join hands and be heart to heart and play a symphony of human civilization together. We should make full use of the resources of the state, the education system and the private sector, make full use of China's advantages in the development of basic education, provide high-quality teaching equipment, overall teaching programs and supporting teacher training assistance to countries along the "One Belt and One Road" routes, and provide high-quality basic education and learning opportunities for foreigners who want to study in China. In August 2016, the Ministry of Education issued a let all the way "area" vision and action takes root in the field of education, the Ministry of Education officials will "promote to build" area "education campaign" a reporter asked how the education action from domestic institutional guarantee to build "area" formation resultant force of education act, article 3 points out that the schools at all levels and orderly. Schools at all levels and of all types are required to expand cooperation and exchanges with schools in countries along the Belt and Road in an orderly manner, integrate high-quality resources to go global, select high-quality resources to bring in, and jointly improve the level of education internationalization and serve to build "One Belt and One Road" capabilities. As more and more overseas Chinese go to work in foreign countries, international schools that serve overseas Chinese will also be put on the agenda. So far, there are only a few so-called Chinese international schools or Chinese international schools in foreign countries. China international school or the Chinese international school is different from our country or overseas education group, primary and middle schools, the school may also be learning the local language and culture, so that students adapt to local life and culture, but mainly adopts the system of education, curriculum and teaching material, for the students to continue to accept education to prepare or take-home examination. With advancement of the strategy of "area" and the "area" all the way along the increase of the national expatriates in China, our government and the social from all walks of life must be put in the "area" all the way along the country to set up Chinese international school mentioned the agenda, the domestic some primary and middle schools should be in curriculum development, teaching staff, management team construction and so on positive support. The report to the 19th National Congress of the Communist Party of China points out that we will advance major-country diplomacy with Chinese characteristics in an all-round, multi-tiered, and multi-dimensional way to create favorable external conditions for China's development. There have also been some changes in the way China conducts its diplomacy, such as education diplomacy. The object of public diplomacy is the whole foreign public, while the object of education diplomacy lays more emphasis on the young students who can play a long-term role in the future. Therefore, the demand for international schooling of basic education arises at the historic moment (Li & Duan, 2019; Song & Liu, 2019; Sun, 2009; Wang & Wang, 2016; Zhou, 2017).

5.2   The Policy Analysis of Basic Education Going Out

5.2.1   The Policy Background of Basic Education Going Global

"One Belt and One Road" construction provides a rare historical opportunity for Chinese colleges and universities to "go out" and carry out multi-level overseas education. While expanding the absorption of students from countries along the Belt and Road, colleges and universities should also make good use of various resources and channels of China's higher education, increase efforts in running schools abroad, establish universities or branch schools in countries along the Belt and Road, cooperate with foreign universities to award double degrees, spread Chinese culture, and expand the influence of Chinese colleges and universities. So far, more than a dozen countries along the "One Belt and One Road" routes, including Kazakhstan, Pakistan, Jordan and Egypt, have invited China to run schools abroad. At present, higher education is going abroad, while less basic education. However, the quality of China's basic education is well-known all over the world. It is necessary and advantageous for basic education to go abroad. The basic education is the enlightening education that lays the foundation of life. The goal orientation and running level of the basic education determine the future of the individual and the country to a certain extent. The comprehensive promotion of "One Belt and One Road" initiative not only requires higher education and vocational education to provide intellectual guarantee, but also the foundation and guidance of basic education in the process of educating people cannot be ignored. On April 30, 2016, issued by the Ministry of Education issued about my state of do a good job of education in the new period open several opinions insist on open still wider to the outside world And stronger Chinese education, puts forward the foreign educational efficiency improved significantly, the education level of standardization and legalization of opening to the outside world has improved significantly, better meet the demand of the people diversification, high quality education, better services for economic and social development of the country. On July 13, 2016, the Ministry of Education issued the Education Action to Promote the Co-construction of the "Belt and Road" clearly pointed out that "China will persistently adhere to the opening up of education to the outside world and deeply integrate into the trend of world education reform and development. To promote the common prosperity of "One Belt and One Road" education is not only necessary to strengthen mutually beneficial cooperation with other countries along the Belt and Road in education, but also necessary to promote China's education reform and development. China is willing to shoulder more responsibilities and obligations within its capacity and make greater contributions to the great development of education in the region." In education and cultural exchanges and common development, the Chinese have the confidence to win "neighborhoods" all the way along the countries' respect for Chinese education culture, the recognition and affirmation, the Chinese have the confidence, responsibility and ability to provide education for "neighborhoods" all the way along the national wisdom and education experience and practical solutions, so as to promote the spread of education and cultural achievements and sharing. The opening up of education to the outside world is comprehensive, including not only higher education, vocational education, but also basic education. In 2018, the Ministry of Education issued a reply to the First Session of the 13th National Committee of the Chinese People's Political Consultative Conference (CPPCC) Proposal No. 3664 (Education 331), which clearly affirmed the importance of opening international schools with Chinese characteristics in key foreign cities as soon as possible and further promoting the internationalization of education. In February 2019, the party central committee and the State Council issued "the modernization of Chinese education 2035, focused on the outstanding problems and weakness of the education development, based on the current and long-term perspective and focus on deployed for the ten major strategic task of education modernization, including 9, put forward creating education new pattern of opening to the outside world, made solid progress" in education action, at the same time made clear to speed up the construction of the overseas international school with Chinese characteristics. In the same month, the General Office of the CPC Central Committee and the General Office of the State Council issued the Implementation Plan for Accelerating Education Modernization (2018–2022), which clearly pointed out the ten key tasks for promoting education modernization. One of the tasks is to promote the joint construction of "One Belt and One Road" education. We will speed up the training of high-level international talents, improve policies for overseas students returning to China to start businesses and find employment, improve the quality of Chinese-foreign cooperation in running schools, and improve the mechanisms for access to and withdrawal from Chinese-foreign cooperation in running schools. We will strengthen education cooperation with the "One Belt and One Road" count One Belt and One Road, build a "BBB1" comprehensive platform for education resources and information service, and establish an international platform for scientific and educational cooperation and exchange. In October 2019, the Ministry of Education issued a letter (Education Proposal [2019] No. 76) in response to the Second Session of the 13th National Committee of the Chinese People's Political Consultative Conference (CPPCC) Proposal No. 3429 (Education Proposal No. 393). Article 3 explicitly proposed to explore and promote the construction of international schools in China on the basis of the existing overseas Chinese education forces. Pointed out that the next step at the same time, the education department under the State Council in conjunction with the Ministry of Foreign Affairs, Ministry of Finance, such as the united front department, we will continue to do the top design, overseas Chinese school in accordance with the timetable and roadmap, pushing overseas Chinese international school pilot work, basic education in China to the world, meet the demand of expatriate children education taking concrete steps forward. In October 2019, an academic seminar on serving "One Belt and One Road" basic education was held in the affiliated school of BFSU. This conference focused on the basic eucaine Belt And One Road under the "BBB1" initiative, closely followed the One Belt and One Road education policy and the "BBB2" One Belt And One Road, and enriched the connotation of "serving" BBB3 "basic education communication. Accelerate the exploration of basic education opening to the outside world, accumulate the experience of basic education going out; The aim is to promote the co-construction, symbiosis and sharing among "serving" basic education institutions, and to promote the modernization of basic education. In June 2020, the Ministry of Education of eight departments to accelerate and expand the new era of education opening to the outside world views" (hereinafter referred to as"opinions") and put forward to in the field of basic education, to strengthen the international understanding education of primary and secondary schools, help students foster a sense of community of human destiny, cultivation of art develop in an all-round way and with international vision in a new era of youth (Li & Duan, 2019; Song & Liu, 2019; Sun, 2009; Wang & Wang, 2016; Zhou, 2017).

5.2.2 Practical Activities Related to Basic Education Going Global (Policy Implementation)

In September 2006, Chinese International School (Singapore) was established. It is the first Chinese international school set up outside China by a private educational institution in China, and the first full-time school with kindergarten, primary school and middle school, mainly engaged in basic education, invested by a Chinese educational institution in a foreign country. The investor of China International School is Beijing Huia Education Institute, which was founded in 1993. Huia Education Institute runs Beijing Huia School, a private school from pre-school to high school. It is also the only school to directly use Chinese language textbooks from domestic schools to teach Chinese courses. "From entering to going out", Huia Education Institute started a bold attempt to introduce Chinese education to the world and achieved important results. While state-funded overseas schools are being built, China's local private capital first expands its brand by opening overseas campuses. Take Maple Leaf Education Group as an example. As of October 2018, Maple Leaf Education Group has opened 91 Maple Leaf International Schools in 22 cities at home and abroad. Its overseas schools, Maple Leaf International School in Richmond and Maydew, Canada, have opened.

On November 3, 2017, the 2nd "Xisha Forum" and the Seminar on "Deepening Basic Education Reform by Integration with 'One Belt and One Road'", sponsored by Shandong Xisha Education Forum and undertaken by Shandong 271 Education Group, was held in Xisha of Weifang. The meeting also reflects the positive change and response of our basic education under the initiative of One Belt and One Road in practice. On June 20, 2019, Minister of Education Chen Baosheng met with visiting UAE Minister of Education Hussein Hamadi and his delegation. Chen made positive comments on the achievements of China-Arab educational exchanges and cooperation. The two sides exchanged views on deepening cooperation in language teaching, promoting two-way student exchanges, discussing the establishment of Chinese overseas international schools in Afghanistan and strengthening communication on education policies.

The signing ceremony of the MOU on academic publishing and educational exchanges between China and Malaysia was held in Beijing on July 9, 2019. The Minister of Education of Malaysia, Mr. Ma Chi-li, witnessed the signing of the school building agreement between the Chinese Cultural Center of Malaysia and Zhimao-mang (Beijing) Education Consulting Co., Ltd. to jointly promote the construction of China International School in Malaysia. As a gift project for the 70th anniversary of the founding of the People's Republic of China and the 45th anniversary of the establishment of diplomatic relations between China and Malaysia, the China International School in Malaysia is located in an advantageous geographical location with complete living facilities and convenient transportation. At the same time, it is the first Chinese international school in the world, and the first overseas pilot of Chinese education going out. It provides high quality and distinctive Sino-British dual-track education for overseas students, trains overseas excellent Chinese talents, and builds a bridge and springboard for students from both home and abroad to study abroad.

In July 2019, the Chinese People's Political Consultative Conference (CPPCC) in Jinan held its fifteenth special topic "Consultation" with the title of "An International Spring City Calls for More Open Education". Mr. Liu, the deputy director of Jinan Education Bureau, announced a good news to the public: "China is going to build the first overseas Chinese international school in Brazil recently, and the only teachers for this international school are in Jinan. Through the construction of overseas international schools, we can extend Chinese culture and Chinese education to overseas countries." Its main purpose is to realize the extension of compulsory education for Chinese citizens overseas. It is the first full-time Chinese international school to adopt the Chinese syllabus for basic education. In 2019, as a pilot stage, the Ministry of Education designated Jinan as the first docking city of China International School in Rio de Janeiro, Brazil. Excellent teachers will be selected and sent by Jinan Education Bureau to support the education and teaching work of China International School in Rio de Janeiro, Brazil. Chinese consul general pointed out as well as in Rio DE janegirl, Rio the establishment of the Chinese international school for overseas Chinese education needs group provides professional Chinese education resources, help to promote humanistic cultural exchanges, and their host countries in China have helped to promote Chinese education, solve the overseas and ethnic Chinese and Chinese children go to school abroad, read Chinese enterprise reality problem. China International School in Rio de Janeiro, Brazil, is the first international school in South America to adopt Chinese immersion education and Chinese teaching syllabus in the basic education stage. The school has far-reaching significance (Li & Duan, 2019; Song & Liu, 2019; Sun, 2009; Wang & Wang, 2016; Zhou, 2017).

On May 8, 2020, the official website of Hangzhou No. 2 Middle School released the news of the establishment of Dubai Campus. In order to carry out the spirit of General Secretary Xi Jinping's important speech "education goes global", China International School Dubai, commissioned by the Ministry of Education and undertaken by Hangzhou Education Bureau, will officially open this September. The school is one of the first overseas Chinese international school pilot units of the Ministry of Education. With the support of the Ministry of Education of China, the Department of Education of Zhejiang Province, Hangzhou Education Bureau, the Consulate General of China in Dubai, the Dubai Social Development Bureau, the Dubai Education and Human Resources Bureau, and Hangzhou No. 2 Middle School of Zhejiang Province, the preparation for the establishment of China International School Dubai has been fully promoted. At present, the preparatory team of the school has carried out a number of preparatory works to ensure that the school can recruit students in June and officially open in September. China International School Dubai (CIDS) is a non-profit full-time school covering 14 years of kindergarten, primary school, junior high school and senior high school. The planned size of the school is 800 students. The primary school is scheduled to open this autumn and will enroll students from grades 1 to 5, with the enrollment expanding year by year. Dubai international school in China "aspire to, hard," as the motto, thought that Dubai's overseas Chinese children to provide quality Chinese basic education for the purpose of the education, so as to meet the future transfer to local Chinese students continue to study or to the actual demand of international colleges, is an overseas student, casting the soul of engineering but also the people's livelihood project of Dubai Chinese, overseas Chinese.

On September 1st, the opening ceremony of Dubai China School was held simultaneously in Hangzhou and Dubai via video link. Dubai China School is one of the first Chinese schools established overseas by the Ministry of Education of the United Arab Emirates. It is the first overseas basic education Chinese international school entrusted by the Ministry of Education to undertake by Hangzhou City of Zhejiang Province and led by Hangzhou No. 2 Middle School. Shang Ke, principal of Hangzhou No. 2 Middle School, said, "As the first full-time overseas Chinese school, it shoulders the important mission of Chinese education going global. There are more than 300,000 Chinese people in Dubai. The establishment of this school will also be a good way to provide Chinese children with better basic education services in China." At the same time, deputy director-general of the Zhejiang province department of education in young said, according to China's basic education school system, curriculum design is given priority to with full-time courses in China, primary and secondary schools in Zhejiang province opened his full current courses (including courses) of all disciplines, at the same time according to the local administrative department of education requirements Dubai, Dubai local courses (such as Arabic, sociology, ethics, etc.) and some of the international course. A series of practices are great attempts and practices of education going out in the international context, aiming to tell Chinese stories well, export excellent culture, improve the country's cultural soft power, and facilitate the education of Chinese children to increase their sense of cultural pride and identity to the motherland. At the same time, it also provides a kind of international dialogue and exchange channel and platform for basic education (Li & Duan, 2019; Song & Liu, 2019; Sun, 2009; Wang & Wang, 2016; Zhou, 2017).

5.3 Policy Issues of Basic Education Under the International Background of One Belt and One Road

In the process of going out, basic education has made some achievements, but it also faces some problems in the process of implementation. This is largely because current policies are not ready.

First, it seems that the number of international schools established by China in foreign countries is relatively small, which is far from enough compared with other countries. The lack of quantity is not conducive to our education "going out". The policy for overseas running of basic education has not yet been issued. "Going out" of basic education is a basic and important step. Current higher education and professional education of "going out" of school based education than the number of "going out" school, more than basic education in the development of international school is good, on April 30, 2016, issued by the Ministry of Education issued about my state of do a good job of education in the new period open several opinions insist on open still wider to the outside world And stronger Chinese education, puts forward the foreign educational efficiency improved significantly, made clear that by encouraging schools and vocational colleges to cooperate with enterprises to go out, encourage social forces to participate in the overseas education, yet prudently proceed with overseas education. But obviously we can see that there is a lack of encouraging policies for elementary education schools to go out. Therefore, we should also increase the pace of "going out" of basic education. In fact, compared with higher education institutions and vocational colleges, China's basic education enjoys a higher reputation in the world, and there will be a need to strengthen the cooperation in running basic education. Our government should support some high-level and distinctive primary and secondary schools to go abroad, set up branch schools in "One Belt and One Road" countries or cooperate in the development of teaching resources and projects. We will encourage more primary and secondary schools to "go global", stimulate the vitality of education abroad, and serve overseas Chinese to a greater extent.

Second, at present, the central government has few policies, and the corresponding local policies are not enough. At present, the "going out" education is mainly higher education and vocational education, and the basic education field is relatively weak or lacking. Moreover, the policy for One Belt and One Road basic education to go out has not yet been issued, which to a certain extent also limits the enthusiasm of some excellent primary and secondary schools to go out. Due to the lack of policies, some schools do not dare to open international schools overseas. At the same time, due to unclear local policies, these outstanding primary and secondary schools also lack policy guidance for opening international schools overseas.

Third, the policy lacks the requirements for teachers and the policy guidance documents for the construction of the corresponding teacher team. At present, it seems that the "going out" basic education has a relatively weak teacher force under the background of One Belt And One Road. Dubai School of Hangzhou No. 2

Middle School sent 3 teachers to carry out education, teaching and guidance, and there was a shortage of teachers. In view of the area along the background, the basic education of "going out" teachers' strength weak, basic education to "go out" really high to the requirement of teachers, teachers should not only to local basic education has profound knowledge and skills, but also to understand the cultural background of the walk out of the country, such as religious background, social background, so in the process of "going out", to avoid cultural and religious conflict. We should understand the knowledge base and cognitive characteristics of "local" students and teach them according to their aptitude. The situation of basic education in each country is different. Primary and secondary school teachers who serve the construction of One Belt And One Road should also have a good understanding of the historical development and trend of basic education in overseas countries where the school is running.

Fourth, the development of curriculum system is insufficient. Based on the perspective of international education to carry out the "area" under the background of education practice, the more concentrated in the higher education and vocational education at the present stage, and mainly students training, teaching Chinese as a foreign language, the basic education stage of cultivating talents of "area" course and research exploration is still in its infancy, and failed to form a multidisciplinary integration research, design, basic education students to develop a comprehensive reading or limited teaching material achievements, the course system has not formed. The curriculum needs to be differentiated and targeted.

Fifth, culture clash. Cultural exchange is the basis and premise of constructing "One Belt and One Road" community. There are many countries along the Belt and Road. Religions such as Christianity, Buddhism, Islam and Judaism are distributed here, and many civilizations of the world meet here. Due to the diverse cultural differences of ethnic groups as an objective existence, combined with the compound influence of various historical problems and realistic dilemmas, the construction of "One Belt and One Road" still faces many adverse factors and cultural resistance. Especially, the cultural stranger, cultural estrangement and cultural conflict caused by cultural diversity make it a new mission for the educational reform and develop-ment of all countries and regions in the world to enhance cultural exchanges, deepen cultural understanding and realize cultural symbiosis. Cultural diversity should not be used as an excuse for cultural estrangement, strangeness and hegemony. The basic education curriculum reform has a special mission that cannot be avoided. At the same time, cultural diversity for the elementary education curriculum reform provides rich resources, we should not only focus on the global mainstream culture, also want to focus on the resources of rich and colorful ethnic culture, should not only focus on inheritance and carry forward the national culture, also should draw lessons from the other culture essence, through cultural accommodation, dissolve the misunderstanding, increase trust. Cultural mutual understanding forms the basis and bond of mutual understanding in all aspects. On the contrary, cultural differences and misunderstandings will cause communication obstacles and even lead to conflicts. There are many countries along the "One Belt and One Road" route, each of which has different cultures, religions, beliefs and customs. Mutual understanding, tolerance, mutual respect and adaptation are all the more necessary in exchanges and cooperation (Li & Duan, 2019; Song & Liu, 2019; Sun, 2009; Wang & Wang, 2016; Zhou, 2017).

5.4 Suggestions on Promoting the Development of Basic Education Under the Background of One Belt and One Road

In view of some problems faced by the development of basic education under the background of One Belt and One Road, this paper puts forward the following specific countermeasures and suggestions, hoping to promote or optimize the international development of basic education, promote excellent primary and secondary schools to go abroad, optimize the environment for cross-border education, and tell a good story of China.

5.4.1 Improve the Quality of Local Basic Education

The realization of the core task and goal of education opening to the outside world is always inseparable from the improvement of domestic education quality. Whether it is internationalizing in China, attracting overseas students, training talents for countries along the Belt and Road, or building Windows for opening education to the outside world, the quality of education outside China is nothing. China's education development level has been steadily improved in the reform in recent years, but there are still many challenges in carrying the "One Belt and One Road" education opening action. In face of the urgency of the challenges, we should enhance the improvement of domestic education quality. Therefore, it is necessary to deepen internal reform to boost the connotation development of basic education. The emphasis on connotative development means that the emphasis of educational reform begins to shift from external to internal, from macro to school, from creating conditions to reforming practice. Its core purpose is to improve the overall quality of students through deepening educational reform. However, it is a difficult transformation process from relying on administrative orders and regulations to independent creation that the reform subjects at different levels carry out the educational reform with the purpose of improving the overall quality of students. With the downward shift of the reform focus, the action subject of the connotative development of basic education cannot always stay at the macro and medium levels but will inevitably move down to the primary and secondary school level as the reform action subject. In the current background, the basic education stage school connotative development, especially should be overcome in the process of reform of three phenomena: one is fixed "within" outside move, the reform just stay on the outside push, pull, actuation, and inside the school did not really start, in other words, the reform has not yet been internalized as teacher development needs and development power; The second is "moving up but not moving down", that is, the reform has not effectively realized the downward shift of the focus of reform, reform is still at the surface, stay in the top-down advocacy, appeals, requirements stage, has not been transformed into the specific work of the school. Third, principals and teachers have realized the necessity and importance of reform and agreed with some basic ideas of reform, but they have not put it into action due to the influence of habitual forces or concerns about the risks of reform. To truly solve the practical problems in the process of the cognitive development of basic education, basic education must be firmly rooted in order to go out, and the local basic education in China must be well managed and developed.

5.4.2   Intensify Policy Publicity

If basic education wants to "go out", it needs certain policy publicity. Current area has achieved fruitful results, all the way in economy, science and technology, education and other fields, but the basic education of our country to go abroad, you need to overseas Chinese to our overseas educational policies have a certain understanding, understand our mode of teaching and school environment, school mission, entrance requirements, etc., policy propaganda need to increase. The "going out" of basic education is finally implemented in the running of primary and secondary schools, and the normal running of primary and secondary schools cannot do without stable students. Therefore, attracting students is an important part of overseas education. We should let overseas parents know about our school and choose our school.

5.4.3   Strengthen Relevant Institutional Support

The "going out" of basic education needs to strengthen system construction to serve the "going out" of education. Pay attention to the institutional guarantee of the construction of overseas branch schools. Although the state encourages universities to build overseas branch schools to realize the influence extension of higher education resources and has issued the Guide for Overseas Running of Institutions of Higher Learning, there is still a lack of detailed and perfect institutional guarantee for overseas running in actual operation. In the field of basic education, there is a lack of Guidelines for Basic Schools' Overseas Running, so corresponding rules and regulations should be improved for basic education overseas running. The lack of guidelines in basic education prevents some excellent primary and secondary schools that want to go abroad from setting up branches or schools abroad, because the leaders of these primary and secondary schools do not know how to apply for school accreditation or locate a school. Running a school abroad involves various departments and requires communication and cooperation among overseas departments. If there are no guiding documents for running a school, these primary and secondary schools will want to "go global" but dare not "go global".

5.4.4 Optimize the Curriculum

We will improve overseas courses for basic education. Under the initiative of "One Belt and One Road", China should not only become the consumer and reference of basic education curriculum, but also become the creator and leader of basic education curriculum. In the process of creation and guidance, the reform of basic education curriculum should reflect national connotation and national characteristics. In order to enable students to practice socialist core values, inherit traditional Chinese virtues and excellent traditional culture, and become cultural exchange emissaries with Chinese feelings, the goal of basic education curriculum should also have a national orientation. At present, under the background of One Belt and One Road, fewer schools have gone abroad for basic education and a systematic curriculum system has not been formed. Therefore, the curriculum system needs to be optimized, which is related to the success or failure of teaching and makes the curriculum more in line with the local customs and culture and the learning style of students.

To promote the internationalization of basic education, excellent teachers are the guarantee. The internationalization of basic education not only poses new challenges to students' ability to adapt to future cooperation and competition, but also puts forward new requirements for teachers to improve their professional quality. These new qualities mainly include international vision, language ability, cross-cultural academic communication and cooperation ability, etc. Language is a tool for communication. Only when languages are connected can mutually understanding and estrangement be enhanced. Only when economic and trade exchanges, mutual learning among civilizations and cultural exchanges can be realized can they be realized. As an important cultural element, language is an important object and guarantee for the improvement of people's livelihood, a media resource for the prosperity of the global economy, and also the spiritual blood of the community with a shared future for mankind. This determines that the construction of "One Belt and One Road" needs language support at different levels. According to statistics, in the 65 countries along the "One Belt and One Road" route, only the official language as many as 53, involving nine major language families. Most of the 65 countries have a single official language in law, with only 12 countries, including Timor-Leste, the Philippines and Singapore, having two or more official languages. Among them, Arabic is the official language (or one of them) in the largest number of countries, with 14, mainly in West Asia and North Africa. Four countries in Southeast Asia and South Asia have English as one of their official languages. There are four countries with Russian as an official language (or one of them), concentrated in Central Asia and Eastern Europe. In addition to the official languages, the number of unofficial languages used in the countries along the "One Belt and One Road" is very large.

Teachers serving One Belt and One Road basic education need high teaching and cultural literacy, which poses a great challenge to teachers. Therefore, more efforts should be made to cultivate such teachers, so as to better serve the cross-border running of basic education and improve the international reputation and influence of China's basic education (Li & Duan, 2019; Song & Liu, 2019; Sun, 2009; Wang & Wang, 2016; Zhou, 2017).

References

Li, J., & Duan, S. (2019). The mission and practice of basic education curriculum under the "One Belt and One Road" initiative. *Science in Contemporary Education, 20*(11), 25–30.

Song, J., & Liu, B. (2019). Promoting the "One Belt and One Road" education opening. *Educational Research, 40*(12), 131–134.

Sun, Y. (2009). Strategic considerations on the scientific development of basic education in China. *Journal of China Education, 20*(3), 8–10.

Wang, H., & Wang, Y. (2016). Language status of "One Belt and One Road" countries. *Language Strategy Studies, 20*(2), 13–19.

Zhou, M. (2017). Rational thinking and approach to the internationalization of basic education. *Management of Primary and Secondary Schools, 20*(5), 5–8.

Chapter 6
Policy Analysis on "The Belt and Road" Initiative for Students Studying in China

This chapter concentrates on exploring the policy analysis on the Belt and Road Initiative for students studying in China. Since China put forward the "One Belt and One Road" initiative in 2013, in addition to the cooperation in commercial trade, infrastructure construction and other aspects, the education cooperation with countries along the Belt and Road has also made great progress. This chapter takes 42 double first-class universities as the research objects, analyzes the policies of universities on studying in China, tries to find out the characteristics and experience patterns of universities' policies on studying in China from "One Belt and One Road" countries, and finally puts forward relevant suggestions.

6.1 Introduction

In his speech at Nazarbayev University on September 7, 2013, Xi Jinping pointed out that "in order to bring the economies of Eurasian countries closer, deepen mutual cooperation and broaden the space for development, we can use innovative cooperation models to jointly build the Silk Road Economic Belt". In the same year on October 3, Xi jinxing, in a speech in parliament, and put forward the "southeast Asia since ancient times is an important hub" Marine silk road, China is ready to enhance maritime cooperation with Asian countries, make good use of the Chinese government to set up the china-Asian maritime cooperation fund, develop Marine partnership, mutual construction "Marine silk road" in the 21st century.

In 2013, Xi Jinping put forward the major initiative of jointly building the Silk Road Economic Belt and the 21st Century Maritime Silk Road, namely the "One Belt and One Road". One Belt and One Road not only plays a huge role in promoting the country's politics and economy, but also plays a key role in the field of education, especially in the international development of higher education. The development of overseas study in the context of the Belt and Road Initiative has promoted

J. Li and E. Xue, *"One Belt and One Road" and China's Education Development*,
Exploring Education Policy in a Globalized World: Concepts, Contexts, and Practices,
https://doi.org/10.1007/978-981-16-3268-6_6

the exchanges between China and countries along the Belt and Road. On July 13, 2016, the Ministry of Education took the lead to promulgation of the "One Belt and One Road" Education Action, which aims to build Bridges for people-to-people exchanges among countries along the Belt and Road, and to provide support for policy communication, infrastructure connectivity, unimpeded trade and financial integration of countries along the Belt and Road. The cooperation of countries along the [] the program will focus on inter-operability education cooperation, training talents, build on the silk road cooperation mechanism, help to develop a broader and higher level, the deeper cultural exchanges and advance along the people all over the world to know mutually close, help countries along the talent cultivation and breeding, to provide talent guarantee for all the way "area" construction, helps countries along the depth study, the thorough exchange, promote the countries along the promote education development, improve the regional education influence. The theoretical design and practice of "One Belt and One Road" emphasize the important role of talents. "Talent is an important foundation and guarantee for the construction of the Belt and Road" (Chen, 2017; Chen & Eliman, 2016; Hu et al., 2020).

The development of "One Belt and One Road" needs talents, and talents are inseparable from the support of education. As the most important base to undertake talent training, colleges and universities are directly related to the quality of talents. Education, especially higher education, should strive to provide intellectual support and contribute valuable wisdom to the development of "One Belt and One Road". [] "Colleges and universities are an important position to realize the" One Belt and One Road "initiative and an important part One Belt and One Roade Alize the" BBB1 "education action. All along, the Party and state leaders of China have attached great importance to the development of the cause of studying abroad in China, which has made important contributions to the reform and opening up and the modernization of education. The Chinese government is trying to build the brand of "Study in China". The "One Belt and One Road" policy of various universities plays a huge role in attracting foreign students and improving the level of the country's education opening to the outside world. By analyzing the study abroad policies of 42 double first-class universities in "One Belt and One Road" countries, this paper tries to find out the characteristics, implementation and problems of the study abroad policies in China. At the end of the paper, the author puts forward some suggestions according to the study abroad policies in China.

6.1.1   Policy Content

In the official website of the 42 "Double First-Class" universities and the official website of the Ministry of Education of the People's Republic of China, the policies formulated by the universities to promote the study in China from the countries along the "One Belt And One Road" can be generally divided into the following aspects.

The top-level design of colleges and universities. The "One Belt, One Road" construction has been added to the foreign affairs strategy of the university, and actively serves the national "One Belt And One Road" initiative. Beijing normal university will service all the way "area" initiative and human destiny community building as a key school foreign affairs work, written to the thirteenth party congress report and "double top" construction plan, the implementation of "area" initiative as the school foreign affairs work, make work plan "area", established to carry out the "area" initiative important position in the school development. Formulate and improve the school's "One Belt and One Road" work plan, strengthen the layout of relevant work plans, One Belt and One Road serve the "BBB1" people-to-people exchanges and educational cooperation. We will carry out cultural and people-to-people exchanges with countries along the Belt and Road, promote the excellent traditional Chinese culture to go global, strengthen two-way student flow and teacher exchange visits, strengthen the training of professional personnel, and enhance cultural exchanges and mutual learning among civilizations.

Colleges and universities establish One Belt and One Road alliance, form a platform for higher education cooperation, and carry out diversified exchanges and cooperation. Xi'an Jiao tong University, Zhejiang University, Tsinghua University, University of Novi Sad, Raman University of Malaysia and other more than 10 domestic and foreign universities as the founding members, jointly initiated and established the "One Belt and One Road" Engineering Education International Alliance. On January 22, 2015, xi'an Jiao tong University initiated the establishment of the alliance. On May 22, 2015, the Alliance was formally established and the Xi'an Declaration was issued. According to the resolution of the Alliance Council, Xi'an Jiao tong University is the president unit and the permanent secretariat unit of the Alliance. So far, 151 universities from 38 countries and regions have become members of the University Alliance of the Silk Road, forming a platform for higher education cooperation covering five continents and carrying out diversified exchanges and cooperation. On October 17, 2015, cultural inheritance innovation high-end conference held in cultural significance in Dunhuang, Gansu province, Fudan university, Beijing normal university, Sichuan university, tong university, Lanzhou university, and Russian Urals national economic university, South Korea and other g8 47 poking university colleges and universities in countries and regions along the "area" release "Dunhuang consensus", decided to set up all the way "'area' strategic alliance" in colleges and universities, to join "area" the strategic alliance of 47 founding universities respectively from Russia, Ukraine, Turkey, Malaysia, South Korea, Sudan, Kyrgyzstan and eight countries of China, Fudan University, Beijing Normal University, Sichuan University, Tongji University, East China Normal University, Lanzhou University and other 211 and 985 universities have joined the project. To build a "One Belt and One Road" higher education community, work together for mutual benefit and win-win results, and work together to improve the well-being of the people in the countries and regions along the "Belt and Road". "One Belt and One Road" Aerospace Innovation Alliance is a non-profit organization formed on a voluntary basis by universities, scientific research institutions and academic organizations in the international aerospace field. It is jointly initiated by the Chinese Society of Astronautics and Northwestern Polytechnical University, and its secretariat is located in Northwestern Polytechnical University. Since its establishment in 2017, the Alliance has grown to 69 member units, covering 22 countries on 6 continents. Alliance in line with "open inclusive, win-win cooperation and Shared development" of the spirit, construct platform for international exchanges and cooperation in the field of the aerospace, promoted from China, Pakistan, Russia, Spain, Italy, Belgium, Argentina, 13 members of seven countries, such as colleges and universities in areas such as composite materials, small satellites and aerodynamic formed five international research team cooperation, enhance member of the union and the international reputation and influence, become an important platform of multilateral international cooperation and communication (Chen, 2017; Chen & Eliman, 2016; Hu et al., 2020).

Colleges and universities are preparing to build One Belt and One Road colleges, strengthen the management and education of students along the routes, and cultivate a group of outstanding young people who know China and are friends with China. Many double-first-class universities actively cooperate with the national "One Belt and One Road" initiative, implement the education action of the Ministry of Education to promote the joint One Belt And One Road of "BBB1", fully cooperate with the opening up of schools in the new era, and promote the construction of "double-first-class" and specially One Belt And One Road for the establishment of "BBB2" colleges. Renmin University of China (RUC) has set up the Silk Road School on its Suzhou campus. The school has made great achievements in discipline development, specialty construction, talent training and cultural inheritance in recent years to carry forward traditional culture and tell the "China story" well. The School has a special program on contemporary China studies, aiming to cultivate interdisciplinary high-end talents and future elite leaders who love Chinese culture and have a deep understanding of China's development path, development model and development experience for countries and regions along the Belt and Road. [], Beijing university of aeronautics and astronautics badious silk road institute was founded in 2017, aimed to response to the "area" initiative in the country, in the "badious navigation" going out strategy play a role of main force, give full play to the resource advantage of Beijing university of aeronautics and astronautics education and scientific research and culture education, integration of the school in students the power of the navigation and location service direction, strengthen enterprises cooperation, face-to-face for talents cultivation, scientific and technological innovation, international exchange, application service four core functions, to create first-class platform for teaching and scientific research, to cultivate more around the world in the field of satellite navigation and related high-end talents, We will promote the application and industrial development of navigation and location services in "One Belt And One Road" countries. Some universities set up One Belt and One Road research institutes, such as Jilin University, Sichuan University and Sun Yassin University.

College personnel training. Talent is an important cornerstone of One Belt and One Road construction. The talents of "One Belt and One Road" related countries are mainly distributed in international trade, computer, finance, language, industrial design, law, civil engineering, financial management, journalism, machinery manufacturing and other majors. The development of "One Belt and One Road" needs to cultivate a large number of compound talents. "One Belt and One Road" needs to cultivate national talents, and international talents not only refer to those who can speak foreign languages. Zhao Lijun, director of the Education and Training Center of China Foreign Languages Publishing Bureau, summed up the characteristics of international talents in the new era into a pyramid-shaped structure from the bottom to the top: they have a world vision and a historical vision; Proficient in foreign languages, master the major; Familiar with international rules; With innovative spirit and international vision. Talents are the key to the development of the "Belt and Road" initiative. Courses that meet the needs of international talent training are offered in China.

In terms of curriculum arrangement, China's dual-first-class universities are actively cooperating with universities from countries along the Belt and Road to jointly cultivate talents. China ocean university is a Marine and aquatic disciplines characteristic significantly, complete disciplines of the key comprehensive university directly under the Ministry of Education, with the cooperation of countries along the "area", strengthen ocean talent training, successively with Thailand, Vietnam, Indonesia, Malaysia, the Philippines, Singapore and other six Asian 10 by science and education institutions established cooperation. To connect with the ASEAN Aquatic Education Network, build a cooperation platform in the field of Aquatic Education between China and ASEAN, and promote the establishment of a trilateral Aquatic Education Community between China, ASEAN and the European Union. China has organized a series of international conferences, such as the China-ASEAN Maritime Law, Policy and Management Forum, the SEI Blue Economy Core Group Seminar, and the ASEAN-China Aquatic Education Network Headmasters' Forum, to play a leading role in regional education and research cooperation. Strengthen the characteristics of Marine talent training, take "understanding China, friendship China, help China Jianhua" as the goal of international student education, take the countries along the "One Belt and One Road" and the offshore island countries as the key areas to expand the source of international students, and constantly expand the scale and radiation range of international One Belt and One Roads from the "BBB1" countries. The "China-Thailand Marine and Aquatic Products Center" will be established to gather the superior resources of multiple disciplines such as ocean, aquatic products, food, medicine and life sciences, and explore international talent training models such as overseas joint training of graduate students. Relying on the existing international cooperation platform, we have organized training programs for senior talents in Marine management and blue economy in Asia, sustainable mariculture technology training for developing countries, entrusted training for international students from Zimbabwe, and senior management training for China and India, so as to build the "Overseas Study University" brand. Beijing University of Aeronautics and Astronautics and Ecole Centrale de France jointly founded the Sino-French Institute of Engineering, which combines the advantages of engineering education of China and France and is honored as a model of Sino-French higher education cooperation. Universities and colleges in promoting union of Tianjin university open courses each other and sharing joint construction course, blue ocean "my dream" summer camp and outstanding senior engineering personnel training mode innovation and development workshops, such as open short-term projects such as communication, access, the exchange students, through the cooperation in running schools, mutual recognition of qualifications, credit swaps, promote the joint training. We will promote two-way study abroad, adjust the structure of international students, strengthen enrollment in "One Belt and One Road" countries, increase scholarship for One Belt and One Road from "BBB1" countries, and support and encourage students to go overseas for exchange and study. Tianjin University signed a memorandum of cooperation with Indonesia's Surabaya Institute of Technology to strengthen cooperation in scientific research, student training and teacher-student exchange, and jointly cultivate international applied talents to meet the needs of "One Belt and One Road" construction. Based on the "China-ASEAN Smart Ocean Center" platform, the Institute of Marine Education offers innovative courses for international students to teachers and students from Indonesian universities and colleges, and establishes a course teaching system featuring Marine cognition, theories and experiments of multidisciplinary cutting-edge Marine technologies, and practical teaching of maritime institutions. We will hold lectures on Chinese history and culture, exchanges on national traditional ethnic festivals, and practice of Tianjin's folk culture for international students to enhance the influence of Chinese culture and promote mutual understanding between the people (Chen, 2017; Chen & Eliman, 2016; Hu et al., 2020).

In terms of cultural and people-to-people exchanges, China put forward the "One Belt and One Road" initiative in 2013. There are 53 minority languages in countries along the Belt and Road, but only 20 minority language courses were offered in China at that time. The problem of language barrier will hinder the One Belt and One Road to some extent. In recent years, many colleges and universities in China have opened minor language majors of countries along the Belt and Road and cultivated a large number of qualified people with language skills and other skills. Sichuan University and the University of Warsaw in Poland jointly build the "Polish +" innovative major to explore a new interdisciplinary talent training model and cultivate high-level talents of non-common languages. Starting from Chinese language teaching, Chongqing University initiates compulsory courses of general education, such as Chinese language, Chinese culture and Chinese stories, for students from "One Belt and One Road" countries, so as to strengthen students' learning of Chinese culture. Hunan University establishes a platform for cultivating talents. We will strengthen the development of courses on Chinese language and literature and culture with Chinese characteristics, develop a comprehensive curriculum system that integrates Chinese calligraphy, opera, martial arts and tea ceremony, develop Chinese language and Chinese culture bases, and train international teachers of Chinese language.

Scholarship system. The scholarship system provides economic support and guarantee for students from "One Belt and One Road" countries to study in China. To some extent, the central government, provinces and universities have formulated scholarship policies of different strength to attract more outstanding overseas students to study in China. At the national level, the Ministry of Education in 2016 developed "promote to build" area "education campaign", will be set up under the framework of the Chinese government scholarship "silk road" of the Chinese government scholarship, the next five years, funding 10000 freshmen of countries along the study in China every year or study, and in the next three years to the professional students of countries along the 2500 people a year. In May 2017, "Silk Road" Chinese Government Scholarship was included in the outcomes of the first "One Belt and One Road" Forum for International Cooperation. In 2019, 54.1% of students from One Belt and One Road countries were studying in China. At the provincial and municipal level, many provincial and municipal governments offer scholarships for international students to local universities at the provincial and municipal levels. Provincial institutions in Shandong, Jiangsu, Shaanxi, Fujian, Gansu, Heilongjiang and other provinces all offer foreign student scholarships of different intensity to universities in their provinces. The municipal institutions of Beijing, Shanghai, Nanjing, Jinan, xi' and other cities offer scholarships for international students to local universities and provide financial aid for international students.

On the corporate level, some schools have accepted donations from certain social enterprises to establish international student scholarships. For example, Wuhan University and Moutai Group jointly set up "Wuhan University Moutai Scholarship" for overseas students from countries along the "One Belt and One Road" route, and Jilin University and Jilin Jindo Group Co., Ltd set up "Jindo Scholarship" and assistantships for international students, aiming to reward international students who are excellent in both character and study.

At the university level, the 42 Double First-Class Universities have also formulated different scholarship policies to attract foreign students from countries along the "One Belt and One Road" routes. Peking University, Beijing normal university, Beijing university of aeronautics and astronautics, Renmin university of China, the Chinese Academy of Sciences university, Harbin engineering university, Dalian university of technology, Xiamen university, south China university of technology, central south university, southeast university, Fudan university, east China normal university, Tonja university, Shanghai Jiao tong university, Zhejiang university, Huazhong university of science and technology, xi'an Jiao tong university, northwestern polytechnical university, Shandong university, Nankai university, Tianjin university, Chongqing university, university of electronic science and technology set up for all the foreign student scholarship, aims to attract more foreign students to study for a bachelor's, master's and doctoral degree. In addition to the scholarships for all students, some of the top universities set up "neighborhoods" all the way along the route for special national scholarship, the reward system of countries along the increase of students, for example, Tsinghua university set up a special scholarship for different regions, Tsinghua university set up Tsinghua Malaysia scholarship, funded study in Tsinghua students in Malaysia; The "Belt and Road" Master Scholarship Program of University of Chinese Academy of Sciences ("Belt and Road" Master Scholarship); Xiamen University has set up Tan Kahn Kee Scholarship to provide scholarships to Chinese citizens holding valid ordinary passports from countries along the "Maritime Silk Road". Xi'an government set up "One Belt And One Road" scholarship for foreign students; Sichuan University set up the "Belt and Road" Scholarship for Foreign Students; Southeast University was the first to set up "One Belt And One Road" scholarship in Nanjing. The School of Management of Fudan University has set up "Xing Quan" One Belt and One Road Scholarship for Foreign Students. Chongqing University has set up a special fund for interuniversity exchange, mainly to sponsor students from "One Belt and One Road" countries to study on campus. Universities provide "One Belt and One Road" special scholarships to provide more welfare policies for students from countries along the Belt and Road, attract more students from countries along the Belt and Road to study abroad, and further improve the proportion of students with academic degrees (Chen, 2017; Chen & Eliman, 2016; Hu et al., 2020).

Cooperation between provincial and municipal schools. Since China put forward the "One Belt and One Road" initiative, many regions have One Belt and One Road joined the "BBB1" initiative. Some regions give play to their geographical advantages to build platforms and radiation centers for studying abroad in a certain country and region. China's double first-class universities actively cooperate with these regions in provincial and municipal schools to make full use of the radiation of the region and increase the influence of colleges and universities. Taking Yunnan as an example, on January 19, 2015, General Secretary Xi Jinping emphasized during his visit to Yunnan that Yunnan should actively serve and integrate into the national development strategy, blaze a path of leap-forward development, and strive to become a demonstration area of national unity and progress, a vanguard of ecological civilization construction, and a radiating center for South and Southeast Asia. Yunnan Province plays an important role in the construction of One Belt and One Road by giving full play to its geographical advantages and relative advantages and plays an important role in South and Southeast Asia. In terms of education, the Yunnan government responds to the "One Belt and One Road" policy and actively cooperates with universities in various provinces to improve the level of education opening to the outside world. Beijing Institute of Technology has carried out in-depth provincial and university cooperation with Yunnan Province. In 2016, the two sides signed the Comprehensive Strategic Cooperation Framework Agreement to deepen cooperation under the new situation and new normal, actively integrate into the "One Belt and One Road", and jointly build a bridgehead for South and Southeast Asia. At present, the two sides have jointly established Kunming North Science and Technology Incubator Co., Ltd. and Kunming Industrial Technology Research Institute of Beijing Institute of Technology., Wuhan university, Nankai university and other colleges and universities 5 and Yunnan province signed a strategic cooperation agreement in 2016, take full advantage of Yunnan in location, resources, the advantage of opening-up, strengthen both in science and technology, education, talent, social services in the areas of exchanges and cooperation, at the same time of power development in Yunnan province, boost the construction of world first-class universities with Chinese characteristics. Chengdu is seizing the opportunity of the new round of opening up to the outside world, giving full play to the advantages of the important node of "One Belt and One Road" and the starting point of the Southern Silk Road, constructing the "Air Silk Road" and "International Land and Sea Combined Transport" double corridor, deeply in One Belt and One Road into "BBB1", and promoting the formation of a three-dimensional and comprehensive opening up new pattern. Sichuan university in Chengdu to build all the way "area" of Chengdu education innovation research center together, boost Chengdu construction of high-level international gateway hub and the inland highland in the west and achieve high quality economic and social development, the construction of Chengdu as the Midwest "area" education research professionals, together with international vision "area" of the education innovation research talents together (Chen, 2017; Chen & Eliman, 2016; Hu et al., 2020).

6.1.2 Policy Features

Promote the construction of the Belt and Road by combining the academic advantages of universities. Some of China's double-first-class universities have disciplinary and professional characteristics, so when cooperating with "One Belt and One Road" countries, they should give full play to their own advantages and specialties to enhance their attractiveness to them. Ocean university of China, Beijing university of aeronautics and astronautics, Tianjin university and other colleges and universities are making full use of the advantages of their own discipline, combined with the national "area" initiative demand of talent training, and other fields with the same forming alliances or cooperation of colleges and universities, to strengthen the precision of foreign students training, promote the development of the professional level. Ocean University of China promotes two-way study abroad, readjust the structure of international students, strengthen enrollment in countries along the "Belt and Road", increase scholarship to foreign students from "One Belt and One Road" countries, and support and encourage students to study overseas.

Universities give full play to their regional advantages and regional radiation. China has a vast territory and a wide range of universities. Colleges and universities in different geographical locations give full play to their regional advantages to serve the national strategy. Universities in coastal areas give full play to their geographical characteristics and actively serve countries along the "Maritime Silk Road". For example, Ocean University of China actively carries out maritime international cooperation with countries along the "Maritime Silk Road" and conducts research on foreign trade between Qingdao City and countries along the "Maritime Silk Road". Colleges and universities in the central region play a role of radiation to the west and south. For example, Sichuan University actively gives full play to the regional advantages of opening to the west and south and "One Belt and One Road" construction and strives to boost the One Belt and One Road of "BBB1".

There are many kinds of scholarships, and the number of scholarships continues to rise. In 2016, the Ministry of Education proposed to set up the "One Belt and One Road" Silk Road Scholarship within the framework of the Chinese government scholarship. In the next five years, 10,000 new students from the countries along the Belt and Road will be funded to study or study in China every year, so as to cultivate leading talents and excellent skills for the countries along the Belt and Road. We will provide more economic support and assistance to countries along the Belt and Road. According to the study in China's official website, the Chinese government provides a total of 7 kinds of scholarship, the Chinese government scholarship includes international bilateral scholarship, the Chinese university autonomous enrollment program, the Great Wall scholarship program, China—the student exchange program, China—AUN scholarship program, BBS program of Pacific island nations, the world meteorological organization project, scholarship variety, large quantity. In addition, many provinces and cities set up provincial and municipal scholarships, and universities also set up related scholarships for different types of international students. These scholarships cover a wide range of countries and have different scholarship policies for different regions and countries. In terms of the types of students targeted, most of the scholarships cover undergraduate, graduate and doctoral students, covering the full range of student types.

Cultivate versatile talents. Domestic colleges and universities mostly establish relevant cooperative relations with other colleges and universities, and actively carry out cooperation with universities with the same discipline advantages. Many universities and colleges have established university alliances with excellent universities in countries along the Belt and Road to give full play to their disciplinary advantages and specialties and strengthen exchanges with different universities in different disciplines, which will help improve the level of specialization of universities and cultivate professional talents. Some schools set up relevant courses to cultivate talents in economy and trade, language, culture, ocean, aviation, transportation and other aspects, paying attention to the cultivation of compound talents and cultivating students' comprehensive qualities (Cheng, 2017; Chen & Eliman, 2016; Hu et al., 2020).

Carry out cooperation between provincial and municipal schools. Colleges and universities sign cooperation agreements with local governments or other provincial governments. Colleges and universities give full play to their own advantages and carry out cooperation with regions with geographical advantages or relative advantages. The geographical advantages and relative advantages of the region increase the radiation force of universities facing a certain region of the countries along the "One Belt and One Road" and attract more foreign students to study in China.

6.2 Policy Implementation

"One Belt and One Road" is a product and bridge of mutual learning among civilizations, in which higher education plays a vital role. Since the implementation of the initiative has achieved a lot of results, China and the signing countries have significantly improved the level of internationalization of higher education.

6.2.1 Implementation Results

In the new era, with the continuous improvement of China's comprehensive national strength and international status, and the continuous improvement of China's discourse power in the international arena, the cause of overseas study in China has made great progress. The Belt and Road Initiative has opened up new horizons for China's opening-up and development. In recent years, the "One Belt and One Road" education action has been deepened and consolidated. In September 2010, the Ministry of Education issued the "Study in China Plan", which aims to increase the number of foreign students studying in mainland universities, primary and secondary schools to 500,000 by 2020, among which 150,000 are receiving higher education, making China the largest destination country for overseas students in Asia. In terms of the number of international students, with the continuous promotion of the "One Belt and One Road" initiative, international exchanges and cooperation among Chinese universities have become increasingly frequent and in-depth, which has built a bridge for One Belt And One Road from "BBB1" participating countries to study in China. In 2016, the total number of international students in China increased by 11.35% compared with the previous year, and the number of students from One Belt and One Road participating countries increased by 13.6%. From 2004 to 2016, the total number of international students in China increased nearly threefold, and the number of international students participating in One Belt and One Road increased more than 7.3 times to about 208,000, accounting for 46.92% of the total number of international students in China. Seven of the top 10 foreign students in China are from One Belt and One Road-related countries. Thailand, Pakistan, India and Indonesia all saw average increases of more than 20 per cent. Obviously, "One Belt and One Road" has become an important growth point for overseas students in China, and the demand is far from saturated, and there is still great potential for growth. Xiao-Hua song and others in 1999–2017-degree students in China national data analysis, in 2017, "One Belt and One Road" along the country a total of 145000 foreign students, foreign students seven states mainly from South Asia, a total of 53000 people, 36 of the total number of countries along the 55%, followed by 10 countries in southeast Asia, foreign students a total of 46300 people, accounted for 31.93%. According to the statistics of the Ministry of Education, in 2018, the number of students studying in China reached 492,000, and the total number of foreign students receiving academic education was 258,122, from 196 countries and regions. Among them, the number of foreign students from 64 countries along the "One Belt and One Road" routes is 260,600, accounting for 52.95% of the total number (Chen, 2017; Chen & Eliman, 2016; Hu et al., 2020).

The number of the students fared better, according to the number of the students can see the top 10, "One Belt and One Road" has become an important market, China's international education of countries along the east Asia and southeast Asia countries the number of international students have been on the rise, especially in southeast Asian countries has been located in the front row number of the students, are the backbone of the area students all the way. Among them, Thailand is particularly outstanding. Since 2013, Thailand has become the third largest source of foreign students in China, and after 2018, it has become the second largest source of foreign students in China. In South Asia, the market for foreign students from South Asian countries has great potential and promising prospects. Pakistan and India have a large number of students studying in China and have been maintaining a good growth trend.

Many double top universities have achieved remarkable results in the number of "One Belt and One Road" foreign students. In September 2013, when Xi general secretary in kazakhstan, first put forward the concept of "area" all the way after school immediately layout in students actively, adjust the expansion of study in Beijing university enrollment plan, the "area" all the way along the country fully investigation and detailed reasoning, set the emphasis on the "neighborhoods" all the way along the route 40 countries of recruit students of high-level platform. The annual growth rate of overseas students is basically over 30%, ranking first in China for three consecutive years. In 2017, there were nearly 2,000 international students at the university, among which students from countries along the "One Belt and One Road" routes accounted for more than 70%. Beijing University of Aeronautics and Astronautics By the end of 2016, nearly 900 students from countries along the Belt and Road had studied at the university and received their degrees. Among them, 182 had received their doctorates. At present, 48% of Bei hang students come from 42 countries along the "One Belt and One Road" route. Chongqing University has implemented the "Silk Road" Cooperative Education Promotion Plan, established good cooperative relations with 40 universities in 13 countries along the "One Belt and One Road" route, and made great efforts to promote cooperation and sharing of academic achievements. We will attach equal importance to exchanges in China and overseas study visits, encourage and support outbound exchanges between teachers and students, carry out the Silk Road teacher training program, and send more than 460 teachers to countries along the Belt and Road to exchange visits, attend academic conferences and conduct post-doctoral research, so as to promote mutual learning between quality education models. Lanzhou University has implemented the "One Belt and One Road" International Student Training Program, receiving 589 international students from 39 countries along the "One Belt and One Road", accounting for 93% of the total international students in the university. The curriculum is based on language teaching, paying attention to the training of foreign students' basic skills in listening, speaking, reading and writing, so as to cultivate compound Chinese talents who are knowledgeable, friendly and friendly to China (Chen, 2017; Chen & Eliman, 2016; Hu et al., 2020).

6.2.2 Implementing the Empirical Model

First, the university "One Belt and One Road" study in China is guided by the national policy. Since the "One Belt and One Road" initiative was put forward by the Chinese government in 2013, universities have actively responded to the call of the One Belt and One Road made the "BBB1" initiative the center of their foreign affairs strategy. The implementation of the policy of expanding the scale of education for foreign students in China is basically synchronous with the promotion of the "One Belt and One Road" initiative. Universities are of course in the service of great national strategies. "Chinese universities have taken action one after another to go abroad and cooperated with the education circles, industry and other parties of the One Belt and

One Road participating countries and regions to jointly compose the blueprint for the cultivation of high-skilled talents." National policies provide good policy guidance for universities to carry out One Belt and One Road construction. "The establishment of theoretical highland makes the construction of colleges and universities between participating countries and regions in a good situation and the flow of educational resources becomes efficient."

Second, colleges and universities to discipline strengths and professional advantages as the starting point. Combined with their own discipline strengths and professional advantages, universities provide precise services for the "One Belt and One Road" initiative and train more professional talents for the One Belt and One Road along the "BBB1" route. Some comprehensive universities, research-oriented universities and universities with disciplinary characteristics can find their own positions and suitable entry points and growth points. For every university in China, the "One Belt and One Road" initiative is a platform for reform and development that they can rely on and live in. While cooperating with the national strategic development and providing various services, not only the abilities of various colleges and universities have been fully and diversified improved, but also their roles and values have been fully reflected. The domestic colleges and universities cooperation of countries along the alliance or related disciplines to carry out the cooperation in running schools or joint training for foreign students to build larger, more open platform for the cooperation culture, actively explore with the cooperation of countries along the resources, countries along the domestic colleges and universities to find and select colleges forming alliances with similar discipline advantage, college students can through the related agreement, in the league to union university communication exchange, through the inter-school cooperation and communication between teachers and students exchange, teachers do share, class sharing, intercollegiate resources sharing, etc., helping each other, promote each other, make progress together.

Third, increase scholarship investment to attract international students. Western universities have also taken scholarships as a starting point in their history to attract foreign students by offering scholarships. "Historically, there has been a precedent in Australia for giving scholarships in order to increase the number of international students for a short period of time. Japan and other neighboring countries compete with China mainly on the basis of scholarships. Obviously, it is a necessary tool to attract scholarships for international students." In recent years, China has provided more and more scholarships for international students, and set up "One Belt and One Road" government scholarships. The government has increased its investment in scholarships, making it more attractive to students from countries along the Belt and Road.

Third, the Belt and Road countries should take advantage of their geographical advantages to study in China. According to Chen et al., 2016, according to the survey of "the five central Asian countries, west Asia, South Asia, eight countries than 19 countries and central and eastern European countries along the 22 countries are higher than the overall growth level, with an average annual growth rate of 37.10%, 30.23%, 25.87%, and 20.95% of the speed rapidly expand the scale of foreign students, and the proportion of the total number of foreign students of countries along the increasing. These geographically advantageous countries, located around China, are significantly ahead of those in West Asia and Central and Eastern Europe." There are also many domestic universities with regional governments with geographical advantages. For example, Wuhan University and Beijing Institute of Technology have signed agreements with the Yunnan provincial government, and Sichuan University has cooperated with Chengdu city to improve the radiation capacity of universities and regions.

Colleges and universities have put forward a number of policies for the implementation of "One Belt and One Road" strategy. Although some achievements have been made, there are still a series of challenges and problems in the process of policy implementation.

First, in terms of the construction of higher education, in recent years, the internationalization level of higher education in China has been continuously improved, and the international discourse power has been continuously enhanced. Chinese colleges and universities are gradually giving out China's voice to the world and passing on China's higher education experience. However, there is still a gap between the internationalization of higher education in China and the world-class universities in Europe and the United States. In the world university rankings, the United States, the United Kingdom and other schools still occupy the majority of the rankings. Take the QS ranking of 2020 as an example, among the top 100 universities in the QS ranking, universities in the Chinese mainland only account for 6. China provides a large number of scholarships to students along the Belt and Road. Many students choose to study in China because of the large number of scholarships and simple application conditions, rather than because of the real strength of Chinese universities.

Second, the regional distribution of foreign students is not uniform. The countries along the "One Belt and One Road" stretch across many regions such as the East, Central, West Asia, Central and Eastern Europe, with wide distribution and great internal differences. Countries in different regions also show great differences in the structure, number and growth rate of overseas students. It can be seen from the top 10 source countries that the source of overseas students is mostly concentrated in Southeast Asia, South Asia and East Asia, while the number of overseas students in West Asia, Central Asia and Central and Eastern Europe still needs to be increased.

Third, the scholarship system for international students is not diversified enough. It is dominated by scholarships provided by the Chinese government, supplemented by scholarships provided by local, private and universities. According to the scholarship information published by the official website of the Ministry of Education, the official website of Study in China and universities, it can be seen that the current scholarship system is mainly based on national and government funding for international students. "The scholarship system for international students is relatively simple, and the Chinese government scholarship is the main channel. A diversified scholarship investment system with the government as the main player, universities and enterprises as the collaboration, and non-governmental organizations and individuals as the participants has not yet been established." According to the information obtained by the author, the scholarships offered by some universities for international students are not displayed on the official websites of Study in China, which makes it impossible for international students to fully understand the scholarship system of universities.

Fourth, the quality of foreign students needs to be improved. The current for national students along all the way "area" a lot of scholarships, but in scholarship awards system imperfect, opaque, and to a certain extent, affect the quality of the students in China, the Chinese government scholarship is not to require the foreign student's too much, some of Chinese and English requirements, but in the students' backgrounds, disciplines scores and comprehensive quality is not request specific indicators, to a certain extent, therefore, the imperfection of the system of scholarship awards. "The state only publishes the proportion of government scholarships, while local scholarships, university scholarships, enterprise scholarships," One Belt and One Road "scholarships and so on, do not have detailed statistics." In addition, "documents from the country of origin of the student are not docked with those from China, which leaves room for fraudulent application materials." First of all, China does not have clear requirements for the admission of foreign students. According to the Ministry of Education's "Management Regulations on the Acceptance of Foreign Students by Institutions of Higher Learning", "the admission of foreign students is decided by institutions of higher learning. Institutions of higher learning shall give priority to the foreign students enrolled under the state plan; Institutions of higher learning may recruit foreign students for intercollegiate exchange and foreign students at their own expense." There is no strict and unified entrance examination system at the time of admission, and many universities have the direct right to decide the admission of students. To a certain extent, it is impossible to strictly and comprehensively control the quality of international students.

Fifth, according to the author queries the Ministry of Education and 42 double first-class universities according to the website, because of geographical and genetic factors, our country in the central, north, southwest of double first-class university actively service "area" initiative of the country, its develop a number of strategies to attract students in areas along the country, in the southeast coastal area of colleges and universities for national strategy put forward by the "area" initiative is less, and the cooperation of countries along the co., LTD.

Sixth, in the context of the normalization of the epidemic, the exchanges between Chinese students and the countries along the Belt and Road are hindered to a certain extent. As a result of the epidemic, the communication between students in colleges and universities cannot be carried out normally, resulting in the blockade of physical space (Chen, 2017; Chen & Eliman, 2016; Hu et al., 2020).

6.3 Countermeasures and Suggestions

First, improve the construction of double first-class universities and build a Chinese brand for studying abroad. First of all, colleges and universities should focus on their own development, accurately position themselves, give full play to their advantages and specialties to actively serve the national strategy, and strive to do a good job in "bringing in" and "going out". The key to improving the appeal of "Study in China" is to improve the quality and overall strength of China's higher education. Teachers level in colleges and universities should strengthen the international teachers' training, improve the level of the internationalization of teachers, improve the level of the internationalization of university teachers is a top priority, and a high level of internationalization is better teachers constitute courses in internationalization, more and more extensive participation in international education exchange, the scientific research cooperation, and attract more talented international students the important basis and guarantee. Colleges and universities should strengthen teachers' foreign language learning, provide teachers with opportunities for overseas study visits, and actively introduce high-quality foreign teachers when cooperating with universities along the Belt and Road. Secondly, colleges and universities can actively build overseas branch schools, realize joint training with foreign universities, improve the popularity of Chinese colleges and universities in foreign countries, and help to attract more overseas students.

Second, the Ministry of Education and universities should establish a multi-scholarship system. Encourage local governments, private individuals and enterprises to set up scholarships for overseas students. The government can provide certain financial aid to local governments or enterprises, provide supporting funds to universities and enterprises that set up scholarship system for overseas students, and provide supporting funds to universities for the construction of hardware and software facilities related to studying in China. Give tax exemption policy to enterprises and promote universities and enterprises to form the internal power to promote the development of education internationalization. In the process of selection, the scholarship selection system at different levels should be fully publicized to ensure the openness and transparency of the scholarship selection system.

Third, establish a strict screening system to improve the quality of international students. Enrollment management is the basis for selecting high quality overseas students and ensuring the quality of overseas graduate education in China, which involves specific links such as admission review and recruitment process. In addition, the relevant departments should make the scholarship selection system public, and the government should establish the professional requirements for the quality of international students and the minimum standard of language level. The application materials of international students should be strictly examined, and the behavior of false application materials should be strictly investigated. The Ministry of Education and other relevant departments of China and the countries along the Belt and Road should cooperate to establish a docking system for the application materials of foreign students to ensure the effectiveness and quality of the application materials. In addition, college teachers in charge of recruitment should also grasp the quality of international students. Finally, in terms of enrollment, Chinese colleges and universities should strive to improve their competitiveness in the international arena, strengthen publicity and enrollment, and attract more high-quality overseas students to study in China. China should strengthen the construction of websites for overseas students from "One Belt and One Road" countries, enrich the content of the websites, provide more distant and rich information for overseas students, and increase the attractiveness of Chinese colleges and universities. "Chinese colleges and universities should continue to improve their recruitment websites to provide objective and detailed information about discipline construction, postgraduate training process, tutors and campus life," she said.

Fourth, improve "fragmented" development and form regional linkage force. "One Belt and One Road" strategy is a regional strategic alliance actively constructed and formed on the basis of fully respecting multiple factors such as geography, culture, kinship, history and economy. Universities with relatively weak geographical advantages should cooperate with regions with strong geographical advantages, sign relevant cooperation agreements, and use the radiating power of a certain region in some countries to promote the internationalization of higher education.

Fifth, change the pattern that the scale advantage of overseas education in countries along the Belt and Road is determined by geographical characteristics in the past, and set up external institutional space and policy environment with inclination and orientation, so as to promote the coordinated development of overseas education in different regions of countries along the Road. Double first-class universities for active service "One Belt and One Road" initiative. Universities located in the east and southeast should actively join the "One Belt and One Road" initiative, and coastal universities should give full play to their coastal advantages to strengthen cooperation with countries along the "Maritime Silk Road Economic Belt".

Sixth, COVID-19 epidemic is still in the abroad, under the background of normalized epidemic, colleges and universities should actively strengthen the construction of "internationalization", the government should be equipped with online teaching facilities in the university and colleges and universities, training teachers' ability to use online teaching equipment, because the outbreak can't timely to provide online learning opportunities of international students studying in China (Chen, 2017; Chen & Eliman, 2016; Hu et al., 2020).

6.4 The Conclusion

The "One Belt and One Road" initiative has achieved great development and played a great role in promoting the internationalization of higher education in China. China has been upholding the construction of "a community with a shared future for mankind". Countries along the "Belt and Road" are inferior to China in terms of economic level. The initiative put forward by China has promoted the economic development of the countries along the Belt and Road, and the cultural and people-to-people exchanges between the two sides have also promoted mutual learning and exchanges between civilizations. In terms of education, China's educational experience has also helped the development of education, especially higher education, in the countries along the Belt and Road. Double-first-class universities in our country have played an active role in personnel training. Chinese universities will continue to adhere to the "One Belt and One Road" initiative to promote the development of overseas study in China (Chen, 2017; Chen & Eliman, 2016; Hu et al., 2020).

References

Chen, W. (2017). Opportunities, challenges and countermeasures for the education development of foreign students in "One Belt and One Road" countries: An empirical analysis based on statistical data of 2005#1#2014. *Higher Agricultural Education, 20*(3), 88–93.

Chen, L., & Eliman, A. (2016). Study on the development change and strategy of overseas education in the countries along the "One Belt and One Road" in recent 10 years. *Comparative Education Research, 38*(10), 27–36.

Hu, R., Yin, H., & Zhu, W. (2020). Postgraduate education in One Belt and One Road countries: Status, dilemmas and strategies. *Modern Educational Management, 20*(5), 51–57.